LIVES
of the
FAMILY

ALSO BY DENISE CHONG

The Concubine's Children
The Girl in the Picture
Egg on Mao

LIVES
of the
FAMILY

STORIES OF FATE & CIRCUMSTANCE

DENISE CHONG

RANDOM HOUSE CANADA

PUBLISHED BY RANDOM HOUSE CANADA
Copyright © 2013 Denise Chong

www.randomhouse.ca

Random House Canada and colophon are registered trademarks.

LIBRARY AND ARCHIVES CANADA CATALOGUING IN PUBLICATION

Chong, Denise
    Lives of the family : stories of fate and circumstance / Denise Chong.

Issued also in electronic format.

ISBN 978-0-307-36123-3

    1. Chinese—Ontario—Ottawa—History. 2. Chinese—Ontario—Ottawa—Biography. 3. Ottawa (Ont.)—History. I. Title.

FC3096.9.C5C46 2013   971.3'84004951   C2013-901519-1

Text and cover design by Leah Springate

Cover images: floral border © Dariara, playing card paper © Alisbalb, old blank paper © Lukas Pobuda, vintage frame © Ryan Deberardinis, floral background © Hcvchou; all Dreamstime.com.
Photographs (front, left to right): Golden Lang, Campbell's Bay, Quebec *Courtesy Golden Lang*; Tom and Marion Hum, and their children, Victor and Wallace, Ottawa *Courtesy Marion Hum*; Betty Joe, Margaret Hamilton, Mrs. Shung Joe, Unknown, Ottawa *Courtesy William Joe*; (back) Harry Johnston and his daughter Doris, Perth, Ontario *Courtesy Linda Hum*.

Text images: floral border © Dariara, old blank paper © Lukas Pobuda; both Dreamstime.com

Printed and bound in the United States of America

10 9 8 7 6 5 4 3 2 1

For my dear friend Diana Lary

CONTENTS

INTRODUCTION

LIKE VIRTUALLY ALL Chinese immigrants to Canada before and during the era of the head tax, my grandparents hailed from the countryside near Canton in south China. My grandfather came as a "sojourner," seeking work to support family he'd left behind in his village and planning one day to take a nest egg home to buy land, build a house and retire. Both he and my grandmother lived out their lives in Canada.

My four siblings and I grew up in the logging town of Prince George in northern British Columbia, where my father had taken a job as a radio operator with the federal government. We were the only Chinese among the families living at the Prince George airport, in housing provided for employees. In reflecting on our experience, I need reminding of our initial surprise at having our attention called—through name-calling and taunts—to our being Chinese. I do remember that it didn't take long before what we had in common with neighbours and classmates mattered more than our differences. I can, however, pinpoint the moment of our arrival in town.

It's midnight on Christmas Eve, 1958. My father, in our 1949 Meteor, drives the deserted streets. We peer over snowbanks looking for 432 George Street. My mother has recalled this street number from fifteen years earlier when she'd addressed an envelope enclosing a note from her mother to a friend working as a chef at a new Chinese café here. We find that café, the Shasta, but it's closed. My father sees staff at the back sharing dinner around a table, so he knocks at the door. The proprietors, Eleanor and Wayne Chow, whom we've never met before, exclaim how happy they are to see some Chinese people and welcome us inside.

The Chinese café, a monument to small-town Canadian life, is a recurring point of reference in the stories in this book. Like Chinese laundries of an earlier time, these restaurants once dotted the landscape across the country. Of course, south China was not full of laundrymen and restaurateurs. Immigrants, facing discrimination and possessing limited knowledge of English, saw these businesses as opportunities available to them. The Chinese cafés initially served only Western food. Not until after the Second World War, when owners were looking to attract more customers, did they offer both Western and Chinese food—not what the Chinese cooked for themselves, but rather "Westernized" Chinese food such as chicken balls and sweet and sour pork.

With time, these restaurants inevitably changed hands. Some of the early sojourners packed it in and returned to China. Sometimes their cafés were bought by their staffs. And when they too moved on, that niche was occupied by more recent immigrants.

FOR MY SIBLINGS and me, our being "Chinese" and China itself, the country of our ancestors, hardly figured in our daily lives. We spoke almost no Chinese and, living where we did, we rarely saw anybody Chinese. Occasionally, we accompanied our father on his volunteer missions to a rooming house in town owned by the Chinese Freemasons that housed a handful of aging Chinese "bachelors." By the early 1970s, these residents were dying out. One was a man who'd been my grandmother's on-again, off-again lover for seventeen years, a relationship I only learned of years later when I was researching my family memoir, *The Concubine's Children*. At the time of his death, I thought it odd that he'd left instructions to send what remained of his life's savings—thirty-five hundred dollars—to his wife and son in China. Clearly, these were people from whom he'd spent a lifetime apart, yet to whom he still felt an obligation. For the most part, such ties had been severed. At the time, I also didn't know that my mother, born in Canada, had a blood sister and a half-brother still alive in China, and neither did she.

In many ways, immigrants and their families conduct life at a frontier, where what was once strange eventually becomes familiar and commonplace. Finding one's footing in a new land and visiting a homeland only in memory is universal to the immigrant experience. However, I came to understand that in the history of immigration to Canada, the clichéd successes of those in my parents' and grandparents' time—of a better life, of moving up in the world and prospering—came for many at a severe price. For them, home and family were one and the same word. They held them to be inextricably linked, only to see events conspire to separate one from the other.

The stories in this book of pivotal moments in the lives of Chinese families are linked to the arc of the immigrant's adjustment to life at this frontier. In exploring how I would document that trajectory, I looked for moments when the forces of history, politics and family combined to bring that immigrant experience into sharp relief.

LIVES WERE AFFECTED MOST during the period from 1923 until 1962. The year 1923 was the beginning of exclusion, when Canada replaced the head tax with the Chinese Immigration Act, also known as the Exclusion Act, which banned Chinese immigration. Sojourning "bachelors" already in Canada could leave and re-enter the country, but they could not bring wives and children to Canada. The law also denied resident Chinese in Canada the right to become naturalized, and labelled all Chinese, immigrants or Canadian-born, as "alien." This inhospitable legislation would remain in place for twenty-four years; by comparison, the average lifespan in China then was about forty years. The year 1962 saw Canada introduce new immigration regulations, which would expand the categories of admissible Asians. That led to further changes in 1967 that eliminated discrimination with respect to immigration on the basis of race or country of origin.

Over those years of restricted Chinese immigration, world events unfolded with calamitous effect. In 1937 Japan invaded China, marking the start of China's Resistance War. That war became part of the global conflict of the Second World War, in which Canada was soon involved. For the duration of the war, all civilian traffic halted across the Pacific. On V-J Day in 1945, Japan's surrender simultaneously ended the war in China and once again overseas Chinese could travel to their homeland. However, peace did not come to China. At war's end, the Kuomintang government and the Chinese Communist Party, which had formed a united front to fight the Japanese, resumed their fight against each other.

In 1947, Canadian Prime Minister Mackenzie King, allowing that exclusion was "objectionable," repealed the act; but, he defended maintaining greater restrictions on Chinese immigrants than on European immigrants because "the people of Canada do not wish . . . to make a fundamental alteration to the character of our population." Canada permitted Chinese immigration again under its "Rules for Asiatics": Chinese men holding Canadian citizenship could sponsor wives and underage children. A brisk illegal trade began in "paper families." So-called paper sons and daughters came to Canada under fraudulent sponsorship; the real offspring were either still in China or had died.

The civil war in China came to an end with the Communists' victory in 1949, which they would herald as China's "Liberation." Like overseas Chinese, much of the population of south China was staunchly anti-Communist. Within months, the Communists brought their radical program of "Land Reform" to the south. The program to confiscate land from landlords and redistribute it to the poor had won peasants in the north to the side of the Communists during the civil war. In the south, the Communists used Land Reform to label anyone standing in their way as landlords or capitalists. As a consequence, many Chinese with relatives abroad had escape on their minds. The British colony of Hong Kong became the all-important, and only, exit port.

In 1955, the Canadian government, recognizing that exclusion had shrunk the Chinese population in Canada and created a shortage of Chinese women, allowed men to sponsor fiancées, a provision that gave rise to "COD brides"—the groom's family bore the costs of the woman's passage and paid "cash on delivery," the traditional "bride price" due her family upon her arrival in Canada. Hong Kong became the major bride market. By the mid-1950s, the colony was plagued by overcrowding and workers laboured under deplorable conditions. Its residents were also eyeing a way to leave the colony for better prospects in North America.

I HONED IN ON THE lone Chinese family and their restaurant in a Canadian town as a way to convey the immigrant experience. Behind that sign on the business, and in the rooms behind or the apartment above, the everyday life of the family would test their ability to adapt.

Fear mongering over "yellow peril" on the west coast had led the federal government to impose the drastic measures of the head tax and exclusion. The farther east Chinese sojourning and immigrant men went, the more they left behind anti-Oriental sentiment. Toronto and Montreal had eastern Canada's largest Chinese populations—still tiny, however, in comparison with that of Vancouver or Victoria.

The families in these stories went farther into the frontier; they settled in and around the Ottawa area, including villages and towns up the Ottawa Valley and on the Quebec side of the Ottawa River, and down to the St. Lawrence River. Ottawa had Chinese-owned laundries as early as the late 1890s, and later, confectioneries and cafés, but no Chinatown (until the influx of immigrants from Hong Kong in the late 1960s). When exclusion took effect, Ottawa's Chinese families could be counted on one hand. In communities nearby, other than the family or two that owned a café, often the only other Chinese in town were bachelors who worked for them.

In Ottawa, these families created a microcosm of what they'd had in China, where some had come from the same or adjacent villages. Evidence appears in the recurring surnames; Hum, for example, shows up frequently. The explanation is in the pattern of migration from villages dominated by one clan; the clan may be able to trace back to a shared ancestor but its members may or may not be relatives. Like a market town in China, Ottawa functioned as a place where Chinese living outside the city came for supplies, typically to one well-known Chinese-owned store that doubled as a community gathering place. And, given the importance of economic fortunes to the immigrant's success, Ottawa provided jobs and created boom times as a result of a growing public service that was required to meet the needs of the wartime and then the postwar economy.

EACH OF THE FAMILIES in these pages is emblematic of the migrant in the immigrant; on the move not only from their homeland to a new land, but from their past toward an uncertain future. Taken together, their stories travel the arc of that adjustment. The path they take lurches—it starts, it stops, even reverses in the face of happenstance and events unforeseen and amid a churning mix of setback and achievement. It may take an entire lifetime or more to see progress, but with each individual family come defining moments that reveal the temperament needed to glimpse and reach for the promise of a future. Each of their stories honours a shared history.

Harry Lim's household in China: (front row) Second Mother (in white) and her son; First Mother (in black) and her children, Fay-oi, and (back row) Min-hon, and his wife.

ONE

ARRIVAL (I)

FAY-OI LIM, RESIGNED TO HER limited choices, selected a white jacket, made of taffeta and trimmed in gold thread, and a long black skirt. Another hand-me-down. Not in the sense of faded colours, frayed edges or telltale adjusted hemlines, but rather of formal wear long out of style. Certainly not something seen in the hallways at school. At least it fit.

She was resolved not to utter a word of complaint. To do so would show ingratitude to the family of her father's benefactor. Lim Jim, a clansman who had been responsible for bringing her father to Canada years ago, was now both neighbour and landlord to them in Vancouver. He owned two houses side by side on Grant Street; he and his wife lived in one and he rented the other to Fay-oi's father, so that Second Mother, Younger Brother and Fay-oi could be installed in a home as soon as they arrived from China. Lim Jim's wife had been unfailingly kind; she came by every day to see how they were doing. She had noticed that Fay-oi dressed for school in mandarin-collared *cheong sams*. When she learned that the teenager owned no Western-styled clothing, she took it upon herself to ask her daughter Priscilla and her granddaughter Evelyn to go through their closets to see what they had no use for anymore, items they wouldn't wear again.

In China, when Fay-oi needed new clothing she asked her mother to buy material and they'd take it to a tailor to be made up. She had assumed she'd do the same in Canada to assemble a new wardrobe—one that would suit the fashions on the streets of Vancouver.

Once here, Fay-oi realized she'd miscalculated.

She knew that her father had spent a great deal of money to bring her, Second Mother and Younger Brother from China. At the last minute—saying he couldn't wait for them to get here—he'd changed their boat tickets to costly plane tickets. But the extent of her father's financial sacrifice became clearer when Fay-oi saw that among the thirty-two students in Miss Howard's class, one of two classes designated for new immigrants at Seymour Elementary School, she was one of only three girls. Few fathers indulged in the extravagance of bringing a daughter from China; sons were the rule. And they didn't move into a house like she did; they shared rented rooms with their fathers. To a one, her male classmates spoke of their eagerness to be finished school so that they could find work to repay their fathers for the expense of getting them out of China.

Fay-oi told herself it was unreasonable to ask her father to spend yet more money on her for new clothes. Regardless, she felt terribly self-conscious.

COMPOUNDING HER awkwardness was her name. When she introduced herself to someone her age who was Chinese but born here, because they spoke little Chinese they would mishear or mispronounce her name. She'd go through the same routine: explain that "fay" was the character meaning intelligent, and that "oi" was the character meaning love. Not that it helped them to remember. They didn't go by Chinese names. Like anyone born in Canada, they had English names.

Fay-oi came up with a plan. It depended on Freda Lim. Twenty-eight years old, Freda was married to Wally, a cook and a good friend of her father's. Fay-oi had a couple of favours to ask. She wanted to make her own clothes; could Freda teach her to sew? And she felt uncomfortable having only a Chinese name; could Freda give her a Canadian name?

On both counts, Fay-oi believed she'd be in good hands. Freda Lim had a stellar reputation as a dressmaker and, being Canadian-born and raised, she could be trusted to choose a name. Freda's early success was well known; at the age of twenty, single and living in Victoria, she'd had her own design and dressmaking shop. Then she'd married and moved to Vancouver, started over in her own home and soon had both Chinese and white customers. In Fay-oi's eyes, Freda was a modern woman.

Freda would have been happy to give Fay-oi sewing lessons, but with three young children underfoot, she couldn't possibly find the time: "It's hard enough for me to keep any regular hours for my business."

However, Freda rose to the challenge of giving Fay-oi an English name. She liked this outgoing girl. She sized her up: tall and slender with a beautiful face, though not in the classic Chinese sense. Fay-oi had an olive complexion rather than pale porcelain-like skin, and freckles. A generous mouth instead of a round one. High cheek bones set off large eyes. Her nose had a high bridge, especially uncommon among the Chinese. Her height and looks must come from her mother, thought Freda. For her taste, Fay-oi's father, Harry Lim, a short man, could best be described as average-looking. His daughter, on the other hand, would turn heads.

"I'm giving you the name Marilyn. After Marilyn Monroe."

Two weeks later, the new Marilyn called on Freda. She couldn't pronounce her name. She explained: "I can handle the letter 'r.'" Normally, the consonant caused trouble for Chinese speakers, but at Fay-oi's private high school in Canton, her teachers, many of whom had been educated abroad at universities in the United States or England, had drummed that quirk out of her. But the equally troublesome letter "l" following on the heels of the "r" was too much: her name came out as Mar-*ri-ryn*.

Freda saw immediately where to make the alteration. "You're having problems with the letter 'l'; we'll eliminate it. Instead of Marilyn, you'll be Marion."

Fay-oi wanted to put her trust in her father's friend.

Freda tried to reassure her. "Marion is a nice name. A simple name, but still, a nice name."

FOR CHINESE WIVES and children hoping to emigrate from China to Canada after 1949, much depended on their performance at an interview with Canadian Immigration officers posted in the British colony of Hong Kong. Officials grilled those applying to unite with husbands or fathers in Canada. They tried to trip them up in order to determine if they were who they claimed to be, to see if their answers squared with the answers given by their sponsors. Of course, the applicants also had to pass a health test, the most important part of which was the test for tuberculosis. Every application stamped for approval helped turn a page of history, granting admittance to the first Chinese to immigrate to Canada in more than two and a half decades.

In the late fall of 1949, Second Mother, fifteen-year-old Fay-oi and thirteen-year-old Younger Brother had presented themselves at the Canadian Immigration offices. The mother and daughter were the only women in the crowded waiting room.

A young official ushered Second Mother and her two children into an interrogation room. She closed the door. She looked at the teenagers. "So you're going to join your father in Canada."

Yes, replied Fay-oi.

The woman asked about their relationship to Harry Lim, typing their answers as they spoke. Impressed, Fay-oi wondered if she too could one day be so competent. For all her nervousness beforehand, the questions seemed routine. The official showed no hint that she suspected they might not be telling the full truth. Fay-oi did not volunteer that her father, Harry Lim, had two wives, or that her mother, the first wife, was not the young woman being interviewed with her.

After thirty minutes, the official closed the file folder on the table, stood up and declared the interview over.

"When do we come back for our next interview?" asked Fay-oi.

"Oh, there's no need for you to come again," the official said. Smiling broadly, she shook hands all around. "Good luck in Canada."

FOR MORE THAN half his lifetime, Harry Lim had navigated a course that he expected would lead him back to China, the land of his birth. Instead, nearing sixty years old—the threshold of revered old age—he was preparing to welcome a wife he'd hardly lived with and two teenaged children, one a son he'd never met, the other a daughter who had no memory of him, whom he'd last seen when she was two.

Fate had plucked Harry Lim out of China as a young teenager. He was born in the village of Golden Creek in the county of Toisan, in the province of Kwangtung. Located several miles inland up Pond River, one of the hundreds of tributaries of the Pearl River that empty into the South China Sea, Golden Creek was nestled into the base of a mountain (it was more hill than mountain, but locals called it a mountain because it rose abruptly at the flood plain's edge). Along the village's ten lanes, squat adobe houses were paired around partly roofed-in courtyards. Larger houses boasted a front door opening onto one lane, and a back door onto another.

Out the back door and down the lane from Harry's father lived the family of Lim Jim, of the same clan but otherwise of no direct relation. At some point in the 1890s, Mr. Lim had left his family and the poverty of the village for Canada, known as "Gold Mountain," where finding work was a prize in itself. A decade later, he returned to China for a one-year visit. During his stay, he took pity on his neighbour's boy, a gregarious youngster named Lim Chung-foon, and offered to rescue him from an unhappy home life by taking him to Canada. The boy's only sibling, a sister, had been given away at birth and he'd lost his mother at an early age. His father, who seemed to care most about imbibing homemade rice wine, had remarried and, as often happened, the new wife favoured her own son.

In Lim Jim's own early years in Vancouver, he had established himself as one of Chinatown's more successful merchants, selling to the Chinese throughout British Columbia. His store, Gim Lee Yuen, carried imported Chinese herbs and dried and preserved vegetables at first. Over time, Lim Jim added goods such as linens, mahjong sets, slippers and dishes to his shelves.

Lim Jim financed young Chung-foon's ship fare to Canada (once in Canada, the boy adopted the name Harry) and arranged payment of the five hundred dollar head tax due upon entry. It was a formidable sum, equal to two years' wages for a Chinese labourer in Canada. The boy proved industrious. From a labourer's job in a sawmill on the banks of the Fraser River, he moved to a job as a cook at a chop suey house in Vancouver's Chinatown and, in recognition of his talents, was promoted to head chef.

After a decade, Harry had savings enough to visit China and stay for about two years. He took as a wife a delicately pretty girl named Chung Yee-hing. Her well-to-do parents owned a successful garlic-producing farm and had promised their daughter, a beloved and only child, to the son of a wealthy family. But after the obligatory background check by a match-maker to confirm the suitability of the union, the young man's parents, suspecting mixed blood in the girl's ancestry, called off the arrangement. Yee-hing's parents had little choice but to settle for a lesser match. Which was how Harry Lim, born into a poor family, came to marry above his station.

With her first pregnancy, Yee-hing delivered the all-important son necessary to continue the lineage. Besides "watering the roots," Harry achieved the peasant's dream of "tiles over one's head." His house, the first to be raised in Golden Creek in his generation, spoke well of his sacrifice of toil abroad. Two and a half stories high and built of brick, the house had modern touches like glass in the windows and tiles on the floors—red clay tiles to warm the first floor, ceramic tiles on the second to keep it cool underfoot in the intense summer heat. A second set of stairs from the master bedroom on the second floor led to the rooftop terrace, which spilled over with potted chrysanthemums. From there, one could enjoy the sunrise and sunset and marvel at the orb of the sun reflected in the wide tranquil river. At the nearest bend in the river, a ten-minute walk away, one could catch a ferry going upriver to the district market town or downriver to the coast, where farther to the west lay Hong Kong, the departure point of ships bound for Vancouver.

Soon after his son, Min-hon, was born, Harry left his family and began his second sojourn in Canada. By now, part owner of a café in Chinatown, he diligently sent money to help support his family. He kept Yee-hing in the style to which she had been accustomed: besides the usual personal girl servant for a wife (even poor women had such servants; to be sold into servitude was often the best a girl from a destitute family could hope for), she had a woman servant who did the housekeeping, washed the laundry, shopped and cooked. And he made sure that Min-hon received a good education, sending him to a school in the district town.

In 1930, Canada began a slide into what would become the Great Depression. China, owing to its silver-based currency, was spared—for the moment. Harry decided to pack in his life abroad; a dollar could be stretched many times further in China than in Canada. In the way a gambler might cash in his chips, Harry sold his share in the café, bid his goodbyes and left for China. As Harry liked to say, "Life is a gamble."

———

BACK AGAIN IN Golden Creek village, Harry added to his family when Yee-hing produced a second-born, a daughter.

Sadly, at age three, the girl succumbed to illness.

Now past forty, Yee-hing defied the odds and became pregnant again. For the second time, she delivered a girl. On the arrival of Fay-oi, Harry expressed disappointment with his wife. "You keep producing daughters!"

Harry still had unfulfilled ambition. "I would like more sons," he declared, and announced his intention to take a second wife—one young and fertile. A wealthy friend of his in Canton arranged to send him a wife from among his seven household servants. At fourteen, Yip Jau-wen was one year older than Harry's son, Min-hon. Yee-hing wept bitterly. Years later she would confide in Fay-oi: "What could I do about it? I could do nothing."

At least Harry had the grace to keep his two wives separate; he installed Second Wife in his father's old house on No. 9 Lane, and left First Wife in the house he'd built on No. 2 Lane. He moved between the houses, uniting his households for mealtimes at No. 2 Lane.

Within weeks, Second Wife was pregnant. The baby, a girl, died just days after birth. A few months later, Second Wife was again expecting.

As Harry bided his time, hoping for a son, he invested in a gambling house with a partner. The venture would turn out to be his undoing; such houses of chance run by men with the "Gold Mountain walk" marked them as targets. In short order, astute gamblers bankrupted Harry's operation. Chastened, Harry pondered how to make back what he'd squandered. He decided his best option was another sojourn in Canada. First

Wife went to her parents for help; her husband didn't have money enough for the boat passage.

With his in-laws' generosity, Harry found himself once again on Canadian soil. His former associates happily took him back as a partner and as head chef in their restaurant business. Devoted patrons timed their dining out for nights when Harry Lim watched over the kitchen. And in Golden Creek, Second Wife delivered her absent husband a healthy boy.

FIVE YEARS INTO Harry's third sojourn abroad, the Pacific became a theatre of war. In July of 1937, in an act of aggression that took both China and the international community by surprise, Japan, for years encroaching in the north of China, launched a full-scale military invasion of the country. Its planes swept down from the north, pummelling China's cities with bombs. By autumn, its armies had stormed into the country's central cities. Foreigners who escaped before Japan blockaded Chinese ports told of the Japanese burning and plundering, conducting mass executions, and murdering and raping at random, including searching house to house for "flower maidens."

A year earlier, Min-hon, by then married and, in the hier-archy of a Chinese family, superior to his mother, had uprooted everyone to the Portuguese colony of Macau, along the coast towards Hong Kong. He enrolled in a school there with a two-year program in Chinese medicine. He had wanted to study to be a doctor of Western medicine, but his English was woefully inadequate. The family enjoyed life in the colony. They lived in a spacious apartment in a large and airy colonial house set in two acres of luxuriant flowering trees and plants.

A servant came every day to prepare meals for the household, do the housework and walk Fay-oi to and from her primary school. As Min-hon's course wound down, however, war reached the south of China. It brought floods of refugees into Macau (the colony maintained its neutrality throughout the war) as families fled their cities and villages ahead of the Japanese. In a place already renowned for its casino tycoons and gangsters, lawlessness erupted. Food shortages worsened. Frustrated businessmen shuttered their shops and houses to return to the comparative safety of their rural villages. Min-hon had to curtail his studies. The war had already cut off his father's remittances from abroad; if they stayed much longer in Macau, they'd starve. Back home in Golden Creek, at least they had their own small garden.

The household divided up, travelling separately. As with every train and river boat leaving Macau, the boat that Fay-oi and her mother took was jammed to overflowing with people and their possessions. The head boatman brooked no exceptions to his rule: "Everybody must sit; nobody can lie down!" His crew pushed on through the night. The constant retching of passengers sick from the fumes of the coughing motor as it struggled against the current kept sleep at bay. Suddenly, a boatload of men, their rifles silhouetted in the moonlight, halted their passage. They forced the loaded boat ashore and ordered everyone off: "Leave everything behind!"

Fay-oi held tightly onto her mother's arm. She wondered if they were about to be shot.

On shore, two of the gang worked their way through the terrified crowd, speaking to small groups in hushed voices. As soon as the boat's contents were unloaded, they said, and as long as no one made any trouble, the passengers would be allowed to return to the vessel and go on their way. Fay-oi buried her head in her mother's chest. She couldn't bear the thought of the bandits helping themselves to her wardrobe of school dresses. However, much greater treasure had been left behind on the boat: her mother's store of jade and gold. Fortuitously, Yee-hing had sewn some cash and jewellery into the lining of the padded jacket she wore.

The family arrived in Golden Creek to find the houses swollen with returning children and relatives. Many had at one time left for the towns and cities to work or open businesses, and now, to escape the rain of firebombs and fighting in the streets, had come back. With so many extra mouths to feed, food was in short supply. Thievery was a constant threat, mostly from desperate residents of nearby villages. The residents of Golden Creek set up a neighbourhood watch at each end of every lane. Min-hon contributed sixteen guns from his father's collection, normally used for bird-hunting. "Who are you? What's your name?" demanded those on watch if they spied an unfamiliar face. If they didn't recognize the name, they fired a shot.

Min-hon and his wife decided that, to relieve the pressure on the family's limited resources, they would head for Canton, where they would take a chance on finding teaching jobs. When Yee-hing's cash and jewellery ran out, she sold her wedding gifts, bolts of wool and silk. Eventually, goods counted for nothing; food could only be bought with cash. When the soil no longer turned up sweet potatoes, people scrounged for edible berries, then roots of wild plants. Starvation claimed Golden Creek's first victims. An old lady and two teenaged brothers, their bodies skeletal, lay dead where they had fallen outside their home. People who'd come from the city told of worse, of piles of dead bodies. Of parents abandoning their children in public places in hopes that someone wealthy might chance by who would rescue them. And of people driven mad with hunger: a mother, thinking her baby to be a plucked chicken, had put it into a hot wok. People believed these stories, apocryphal or not, because they had witnessed unimaginable deprivation and loss.

The villagers of Golden Creek grew anxious, expecting the Japanese eventually to target their village. Sure enough, the day came. Fay-oi, then seven or eight years old, heard a stampede of feet by the house and the tense voices of mothers hurrying their children. Alone in the house with her mother, who was ill and confined to bed, Fay-oi ran outside. Neighbours said the Japanese had struck at the houses clustered at the bend in the river. From the rooftop terrace, Fay-oi saw for herself: a large military boat moored there and smoke billowing from houses nearby.

She rushed to rouse her mother. Yee-hing had not eaten for days and had been coughing up blood. "*Mama,* everyone is going to the mountain."

"I'm too weak." Go, she said weakly. Go, quickly.

"If you're going to die, *Mama,* I want to die with you." Fay-oi crawled under the covers of the bed that mother and daughter had shared ever since Harry left for Canada.

In the stillness of the house, the two clung to each other. They awaited the inevitable: the sound of breaking glass as the enemy broke through the first door, the clang of the slatted metal of the second door sliding across, the smashing of the wooden lock and the creak of the massive timber door swinging aside. Boot steps on the ground floor, then hastening up the stairs. Soldiers bursting into the bedroom. Instead, the silence gave way to the rustle of the leaves and the music of songbirds. A few hours later, Fay-oi heard the relieved chatter of returning villagers. She ran out: Why had they come down off the mountain? They said that from on high among the pine trees, they had seen Japanese soldiers board their boat and move on down the river. They snickered at the Japanese: maybe they were too lazy to make the ten-minute walk from the river's edge to Golden Creek.

Eight years after Japan had invaded China, the occupation ended; that same day, Japan announced its unconditional surrender in the Pacific War, following the dropping of atomic bombs on Hiroshima and Nagasaki. Still, the people of China would have no respite from conflict. Hardly were the Japanese gone when Chiang Kai-shek's Kuomintang government and Mao Tse-tung's Communists renewed their civil war.

AS BAD AS THINGS in China may have looked to Harry, he saw his prospects in Canada only improving. He and several partners had renovated a property on Vancouver's Pender Street and renamed it W.K. Oriental Gardens (W.K. stood for *wah kew*, a term to describe "overseas Chinese"). Richly decorated with wood panelling and rows of tasselled silk lanterns hanging from the ceiling, the restaurant was located up a wide staircase on a second floor, evoking a tradition in Canton that sharing food and conversation is to be enjoyed away from prying eyes and the din at street level. By the mid-1940s, W.K. Gardens had become one of Chinatown's busiest restaurants. Its four-page menu offered Canadian and Chinese dishes, from T-bone steak with a choice of seven styles of potatoes (French fries to potatoes *au gratin),* to nine variations on chop suey. Sundays were given over to Chinese cuisine with a set banquet menu. Waiters rolled out rounds of plywood to enlarge the tables and seat as many as five hundred guests. Several nights a week, the restaurant offered a popular ticketed "Dine and Dance" evening, to the swing music of a big band.

At the end of the Second World War, Harry Lim played a waiting game. If Canada reversed its immigration policy and began re-admitting Chinese, he could think about getting his family out of China. Chinese-Canadian soldiers had supported the British defence of Hong Kong against the Japanese and had paid a heavy price in casualties, both in battle and in Japanese prisoner-of-war camps. China had fought on the side of the Allies, and Chinese men and women in Canada had voluntarily enlisted to help Canada's war effort. The United States had repealed its own exclusion act in 1943. How much longer could Canada hold out?

In 1947, the Canadian parliament relented. It lifted exclusion and restored the right of Chinese immigrants already resident in the country to become naturalized. The government announced that Chinese men who had acquired Canadian citizenship could apply to sponsor wives and dependent children.

IN THE SUMMER OF 1949, Fay-oi arrived home on vacation from her school in Canton. Her mother greeted her, looking grave: "I have a surprise for you." She handed her a letter postmarked from Canada. Its contents shocked Fay-oi; her father had sent instructions for herself, Second Mother and Youngest Brother to prepare to immigrate to Canada. However, he added, "if you're not sure about leaving your mother now, you can always come later, as someone's wife."

Fay-oi evaluated her life in China. No compelling reason presented itself for her to leave. The family had survived the war years. Min-hon had secured their future. He had dutifully followed their father's advice: if and when the strife of war subsides, add to the family's holdings of *mau tin*. Someone could steal a water buffalo or empty another's larder, but cultivated land, which earned rental income, stayed put. But above all, Fay-oi was rejoicing in life as a family unit again. A year or so before the war ended, Min-hon and his wife had moved Yee-hing and Fay-oi from the village to live with them in a district market town near Canton. The couple had received an offer to establish a new school there. The job came with a large house set in a spacious garden with a lemon tree, a papaya tree and an apple tree amid the flowering shrubs. When Min-hon had proposed that mother and daughter join them, Yee-hing packed two suitcases without hesitation, locked the doors of the house on No. 2 Lane and gave the key to a relative.

As Fay-oi saw it, her life already had the benefits of an overseas connection. Theirs was a household headed by a father whose money and attentions allowed them to live well. Every care package Harry sent indulged the women he'd left behind—a petticoat, a crinoline, seamed nylon stockings, leather gloves, once, a fur stole. A rich friend of her mother's, who owned a seven-storey hotel a block from the waterfront in Canton, had befriended Min-hon, bringing Fay-oi into the social circles of a cultured elite. Attendance at a private high school conferred on her the company of the children of doctors, lawyers and business people. How would life abroad be any more privileged than this?

Yet, thought Fay-oi, if she went to Canada, apart from learning English, her adjustment to living in a white society probably wouldn't be that difficult. Certainly, going abroad appealed to her adventurous streak. When she was perhaps eight or nine, she had decided to visit the wife of her uncle. The woman lived downriver in the next village, where Fay-oi had never been. Undaunted, she walked to the river and boarded a ferry. At the next stop, about four kilometres away, while waiting to disembark, she tugged at the sleeve of one of two ladies standing close beside her and asked politely for directions to her aunt's house. Startled, each of the ladies asked her neighbour: "Aren't *you* her *Mama?*"

Yee-hing had waited two days before asking her daughter: "Have you made up your mind? Are you going to Canada?"

During that time, tension had gripped the household. Min-hon, disappointed that he wasn't the one going to Canada, had turned sullen. He'd never lost sight of his ambition to be a doctor of Western medicine, but he understood too that he'd never achieve the necessary proficiency in English in China. Harry had written to explain why he couldn't sponsor him to come to Canada: Canadian rules specified that only dependent children under the age of eighteen were eligible. Min-hon was twenty-nine.

Fay-oi answered her mother with an emphatic yes.

Yee-hing was downcast: "Why would you want to go to a strange country where people eat only potatoes?"

"For two reasons," Fay-oi replied. "I have no memory of my father. And I would like a university education in the West."

How could Yee-hing object? The word *Baba* had hardly crossed her daughter's lips. She and Min-hon had been determined that Fay-oi start school at an early age; she'd bribed her daughter by promising her new dresses—they took her Shirley Temple doll to the tailor so that her frocks could be modelled after the doll's dresses. Even before Fay-oi started school, Min-hon had tutored her in the English alphabet. And for high school, Yee-hing had given her up to boarding school.

Yee-hing said nothing.

In responding to her father, Fay-oi addressed his suggestion that she could come later as a wife. She had found it demeaning that her father would make a bargain of marriage for her. Never would she enter into an arranged marriage as her mother had done; nor could she be bought like Second Mother. Fay-oi made herself clear: "*Baba*, I am coming to Canada on one condition: as your daughter. I will never, never, come as someone's wife."

When the day of departure came, only Yee-hing rose to send her off. Fay-oi felt hurt that Min-hon and his wife did not bother to get out of bed to say goodbye; no one knew when, if ever, they might see each other again.

Fay-oi and her mother stood on the pier waiting for the boat to take her on the first leg of her trip, to Hong Kong. Each remained composed; neither wanted the other to see her cry. "I'm capable of looking after myself, *Mama*," Fay-oi said. "There's no need for you to worry." Once on the boat, Fay-oi watched until her mother, unmoving on the pier, disappeared from view as the boat rounded the bend in the river.

———

AFTER A YEAR AND A HALF studying basic English at Seymour School, Marion—as Fay-oi now called herself courtesy of Freda—scored high enough to be placed in ninth grade in public school at Britannia High. At the end of the tenth grade, she asked her father his opinion of what her future course of study should be at university.

"You're a girl!" Harry sputtered. "Why would you need a degree to stay in the kitchen? You don't need to make a living to support the family. Don't plan on going to university."

Her father's response plunged Marion into despair. She suddenly saw the reality of her life in Canada. Second Mother, who became pregnant soon after their arrival, had delivered a second son; university was an expense to be saved for a boy. And one whose entire schooling would be in Canada, one whose English would always be better than hers. I have no interest in cooking, Marion wanted to say in retort. Something her mother said came back to her: "When you marry, you'll have many servants; there's no need for you to learn to cook."

At the suggestion of the guidance counsellor at Britannia, Marion transferred to Vancouver Technical School to take secretarial training. But she would not be cowed by her father's rebuke. She resolved to take her education and her future into her own hands. Learn English, Marion. Learn English.

Marion insisted that her Chinese school chums speak only English to her. She kept company with them after school, when they routinely headed to one home or another. They'd raid family fridges for pie and ice cream, and then settle into gossip and idle chatter, except for Marion. She asked them to take turns firing English words at her. She would repeat the word, then spell it. She'd sometimes be so focused on incoming words that she wasn't aware she was repeating their conversation—"Holy. H-O-L-Y. Smoke. S-M-O-K-E." Marion made a pledge to herself; never would she stop learning. My father has ended my education; I have not, she told herself.

ON SATURDAY EVENINGS when W.K. Oriental Gardens got especially busy or a private party had taken it over, Harry would ring home to tell Marion to come help out Jessie Kwong at the hat check. Besides taking coats, hats and umbrellas, the hat check girls had to sell cigarettes. Marion relished those nights. The well-heeled clientele kept up a patter with Jessie; everybody knew her brother, Larry, famous for being the first Chinese to play in the National Hockey League. (He would play but one shift. In 1948, the New York Rangers put him on the ice late in the third period against the Montreal Canadiens.) Few knew that Larry had been the only player with the Trail Smoke Eaters (from which he'd been scouted by the Rangers' farm team) who had not been supported by a job "up the hill"; the town's Cominco Smelter had a "No Orientals" policy. Larry had had to settle for a job as a hotel bellhop.

Among Marion's friends, Jeanne Yip, three years older than her, was to her the model of sophistication. Being of the same height and build, Marion liked to imagine her friend's clothes as her own. By day, Jeanne wore smart dresses and suits, with a hat and gloves and shoes to match. By evening, she dressed for her social life. Jeanne had once fantasized that she'd move to San Francisco and be a dress designer in the Chinatown there. Instead, she worked as a secretary to Quon Wong (the province's first Chinese notary), who ran an agency in Chinatown offering interpretation and advisory services, and which was especially in demand for issues related to immigration. Jeanne, the eldest of ten, was perfectly bilingual, for which she credited her parents. They'd insisted that their children not mix English words with their spoken Chinese, a policy that eroded, however, further down in the sibling order.

If ever a Chinese group organized a dance, you could count on seeing Jeanne Yip on the dance floor. (Chinese army and navy vets and YMCA and YWCA members often rented night spots like the Commodore downtown or the Alma Academy out by the University of British Columbia.) Because Jeanne didn't like to wear the same party dress twice, her routine after work often involved stopping at a fabric shop to buy yardage, usually remnants she could experiment with and combine with what she had on hand. She'd look at her file of ideas, sketch a design, lay out the fabric and start sewing. By morning, she'd have a dress ready to be worn that evening.

House parties were the extent of Marion's social life: boys and girls gathered at someone's house, put out bottles of soda pop and potato chips and popcorn, and turned up the hi-fi. The real excitement came before the party, when the girls fussed over what to wear.

One day, Marion attended the wedding of a relative of Jeanne's and gasped at the gown her friend wore: coral-coloured, strapless, with three tiers of tulle cascading to the floor. Marion swooned: "I *love* it!"

"Then you can have it."

At seventeen years old, Marion had yet to go on a first date. For months thereafter, she hoped fervently that some boy would ask her out somewhere where she could show off her new gown. Incredibly, it happened.

A Chinese boy asked if she'd like to accompany his two friends and their dates to The Cave, a supper and night club. Mere mention of The Cave on Howe Street, near the landmark Hotel Vancouver, evoked urban sophistication. On nights when the club hosted big-name acts, the latest Oldsmobiles pulled up in front to discharge socialites escorted by men in tuxedos.

If she hadn't had Jeanne's dress, Marion would have told the boy she couldn't go. The only good dresses she owned were her richly embroidered *cheong sams*. She couldn't wear one of those to The Cave. It would be obvious: the immigrant girl had to go into her trunk from China to find something to wear.

On the evening of Marion's date, at the appointed hour, the boy knocked at the door of the Lims' house. Marion appeared in her splendour.

She had expected his approval. Why, she wondered, did he look so crushed?

At The Cave, they passed under the large neon sign over the entrance and through the doors, and went down the stairs into the semi-darkness of a cavernous grotto with white plaster stalactites hanging from the ceiling.

The boy's friends had already claimed a table near the dance floor and stage. Suddenly, Marion understood why her date was so miserable; the two other girls in their party were in knee-length skirts and twin sweater sets.

Marion and her date sat in stony silence.

Whenever the club's roving spotlight came near, she shrank from it. Every time she looked at her watch, not ten minutes had passed since she'd last checked it. She couldn't wait for the evening to end.

Years later, when Marion moved to the other side of the country and found herself shivering through an Ottawa winter, she'd be amused that yet again she'd erred in what to wear. Coming from Vancouver, she had never imagined the season could deliver such icy temperatures and snow. Never mind, she told herself, I'll know for next year.

Lui-sang Hum during her first winter in Ottawa.
Courtesy Lui-sang Wong

TWO

LAYERS

MANY OF THE Chinese immigrants who had arrived in Ottawa in the 1950s settled near the downtown core. Rents were cheap, owing to all the commerce mixed into the residential blocks. Within a mile of Parliament Hill, on residential streets off busy, shop-lined Bank Street, a handful of houses were home to families, often multiple families, of Chinese origin. On Waverley and Frank streets a pocket of such immigrants lived in the shadow of the cavernous Colonial Furniture. Owned by the Cohen family, the store straddled two buildings: one used to be a turning and lathing mill, and the other a car dealer's showroom for Packards and Studebakers. Colonial's sign, which stretched two stories high and overhung the sidewalk, made it impossible to miss.

For four years, two young women, who had immigrated to Canada within the same year, lived across from one another on Frank Street. They knew each other by name and said hello when they crossed paths on the street. One was married, one was not. One had been sponsored as a bride, the other as a dependent child. They were not friends; however, given how sparse the Chinese were among the city's overwhelmingly white population, if you were Chinese and if ever you passed another Chinese person, you made eye contact and you smiled as if you had known each other for a long time.

One of these women was Lui-sang Hum. She had come at the age of sixteen in 1958. A bright-eyed girl with cherubic cheeks, she lived like a domestic under the thumb of Mrs. Eng, whom she addressed as Third Auntie—the third-born among her mother's siblings. She and Mr. Eng had financed Lui-sang's immigration to Canada. Mr. Eng waited on tables at the Ho Ho Café, and Third Auntie stayed at home with their four young children, all under the age of six. The Engs owned their own home on Frank Street, and from time to time rented rooms out. Lui-sang lived with them for four years, until she married Tsan Wong, a part owner of the busy Canton Inn.

The other was Lai-sim Yee, who arrived on Frank Street in 1959 at the age of twenty-one. She came to marry Yu-nam Leung, a cook who divided his time between the Cathay House restaurant downtown and its owner's second restaurant, the Sampan, out in the suburbs. The Leungs began their married life in two matchbox-like rooms. Their landlord, Mr. Kung, whose new laundromat business was doing well, had turned his fourplex into a rooming house of sorts. A kindly man, he helped many new arrivals with their immigration paperwork. He'd pick them up from the airport and sometimes offer to run an errand in his new Chevy. The Leungs' household expanded: by the fourth year, they would be two couples, each with a child, sharing two rooms, with no kitchen other than a hotplate and the bathroom sink.

In the summer of 1963, Lui-sang moved one block to the north, to Waverley Street. Lai-sim followed a few months later. Their street view was much the same as before—the side of Colonial Furniture and its gravel parking lot. Once again, they lived across from each other. But where they once had been tenants, now they were homeowners, each with her own street address and her own front door. Lui-sang, who owned the larger house, adorned with decorative brickwork, had her own covered front porch large enough to sit in. Lai-sim's plain, even shabby, red brick house, was smaller, but with six rooms—tiny, mind—spread over two and a half floors, her extended household was no longer tripping over one another.

On Waverley Street, a new neighbourliness seeded the ground between the two women. It didn't take long before one or the other could be seen scurrying across the street to visit. Eventually, over the ten years that they would both live on Waverley Street, the hour wouldn't matter, early morning or late—very late—into the night. Nor the elements, rain or shine. Both determinedly beat a path to the other's door. "My sister! My best friend!" they'd say. In English, as if marking the friendship as homegrown, in Canada.

IN THE WAKE OF THE Canadian government's lifting of exclusion, new Chinese immigrants arrived with an identity that was determined by the connection that got them into the country: as a wife or a dependent child reuniting with a husband or parent, or promised as a bride. These identities suggested that the familial relationship was the referee of their lives. In reality family stories set against the tragic and sometimes brutal history of the previous decades had been sagas of loss and dislocation. So, given the opportunity, someone resourceful might try to realign fractures in the family narrative to restore or recast the original, or construct a new one. To do so, however, might compel one to unearth memory. Or alternatively, to bury memory.

"We'll do whatever we have to, to keep up your story, but if you want to stay in Canada, you better move in with us." Chiu Hum and his wife and their two daughters, who'd come to visit Lui-sang at the Engs' immediately upon her arrival, pressed her to move from Third Auntie's to their house. A well-known cook among Chinese café-owners, Mr. Hum warned her of the zealousness of the RCMP: they were rumoured to arrive unannounced to ask to see immigration documents and would take anyone caught out as paper sons and daughters straight out to the airport and put them on a plane—although nobody actually knew of anyone to whom this had happened.

Lui-sang's performance had convinced Canadian Immigration officials once that she was Jin-hai Hum, the middle daughter of the couple in Ottawa who, at the time, rented rooms in Third Auntie's house.

Third Auntie said they should stick to the original deal. A calculating woman, she had happened to hear the Hums, when she'd rented them rooms, speak of a daughter who, had she lived, would be fourteen. She had pounced: How many children did Mr. Hum register with Canadian Immigration? Three; he'd neglected to mention that one had died. Mrs. Eng asked to buy the dead daughter's "slot" for her niece Lui-sang to enter Canada. The girl was sixteen, but being short, could easily pass for fourteen. Besides, authorities likely wouldn't try to verify the existence of a daughter. The birth or death of a daughter was hardly notable, warranting, at best, a slip of paper with a name on it tucked into the pages of a family's genealogy book.

The two families, at loggerheads over where Lui-sang should live, agreed to put the issue to the matriarch of Third Auntie's family. She lived in Stephenville, Newfoundland, having only recently reunited with Lui-sang's grandfather after being separated by exclusion for twenty-five years. Afraid of making the wrong decision, the old lady dithered so long that Auntie eventually got her way.

Within days of moving in with the Engs on Frank Street, Lui-sang met Uncle's mother. She was so affected by how desperately the young girl wanted to find work in order to send money to her mother that the old woman went straight away to talk to the owner of a café where she herself had worked nights in the kitchen. By week's end, Lui-sang was hired to work six days a week, eight to five, at the New Astor Café around the corner. She put in long days, beginning with fixing breakfast for the four Eng children. At the restaurant, besides keeping up with dirty dishes, every day she had to peel a hundred pounds of potatoes, push them, potato by potato, through the French Fry chopper, and then work her way through a bushel basket of raw chicken breasts, cutting them into cubes for the next day's chicken balls. Back at home, exhausted, her arms red and inflamed from the lye in the dishwashing solution, she'd start dinner for the children.

Now and again, Lui-sang would take a detour on her way home from work to swing by her paper family's house. Suspecting as much, Auntie barked at her: "Just stay in the house! You go to work, okay. Go to school, okay. But the rest of the time, stay in the house!" Her niece paid no heed. Whereas she was glum and morose at the Engs', her cheerful self and infectious laugh came back at the Hums. In any event, her paper mother wanted to see her at least monthly; she insisted on handing over to her the proportionate share of the family allowance cheque that she got from the government, payments that would continue until her deceased daughter would have turned sixteen.

Six months into her life in Canada, Lui-sang's paper father spoke to her in confidence. His tone was ominous. "Do you know why you were brought to Canada?" She repeated what she'd been told in Hong Kong; her Stephenville grandfather told her mother to send her to Canada to mind Third Auntie's children: "Third Auntie needs to go outside to work to get more money."

"That's not why. I'll tell you why. You babysit for a while and then when you're older, you apply to get your Auntie's youngest brother to come here to be your husband."

Several months later, Mr. Hum brought happy news to Lui-sang: her grandmother had found a bride—a girl in Newfoundland—for her uncle. I'm so lucky, realized Lui-sang. Perhaps fate had taken its first turn in her favour. She redoubled her efforts to learn English. In addition to taking night school classes for new immigrants, she signed up for the remedial English class at the Chinese Christian Mission. Miss Ricker, the deaconess, a former missionary now in her sixties, held sessions on Wednesday evenings and Sunday afternoons; Lui-sang showed up on Sundays, joining six or seven others. When Third Auntie came upon Lui-sang's notebooks, she collected them and told her children to tear them up. Lui-sang wondered if her aunt feared she'd better herself too quickly.

LAI-SIM YEE FELT ONLY indifference when told by her grandmother that she was to be sent to Canada to marry. In the five years since her arrival in Hong Kong she had never felt comfortable. Having lived only a rural life and speaking her village dialect, she felt others, with their urban ways and their refined Cantonese, looked down on her. Neither did she feel at home with her extended family in Hong Kong; she was the daughter of First Mother who died years before. But she was as much an outsider because she had "gone out"; a girl who has left her birth family, usually by marriage but in her case because she was adopted out, does not return.

As the one who'd given her granddaughter away the first time, the old lady had no qualms about doing it again. She saw her chance when Canada introduced a program in 1955 allowing Chinese men in Canada holding Canadian citizenship to sponsor a fiancée. Lai-sim knew nothing of the man she was to marry, only that her grandmother and his had concluded a deal to send her as a COD bride.

On December 10, 1959, eight days after Lai-sim arrived in Ottawa (the program's rules specified that a marriage had to take place within thirty days), she married Yu-nam Leung, a thin man whose subdued manner was the opposite of her chatty nature. The couple moved into Mr. Kung's rooming house on Frank Street. Ten months later, they had a squawling infant boy, Billy.

Lai-sim's experience in Canada echoed the isolation she'd felt in Hong Kong. At first, she'd felt hemmed in by the cold and her fear of slipping on the snow and ice. Then, more so by her lack of English. When she did venture out with Billy, knowing she wouldn't be able to ask directions never mind comprehend the answer, she circled the same nearby blocks.

Yu-nam's fourteen hour days at his dishwashing job left Lai-sim only the company of the baby. Her one slim hope of turning up something lucky in Canada seemed to have evaporated. She'd written to an address in Altona, Manitoba, to the husband of the grandmother who'd sent her abroad. She asked after an older brother from her birth family, named Mun-fei, whom she understood to have gone to work for him. If the family in Hong Kong was hostile towards her, perhaps, throught Lai-sim, the siblings she had yet to meet might feel differently. When no reply came, she tried again. She wondered if her rudimentary Chinese was the problem; she'd had only a fifth-grade education. Again she received no response.

When Billy was only months old, Lai-sim received news of Mun-fei. A brother-in-law in Canada told her that Mun-fei had moved to Winnipeg, and that he went by the name Henry. The two siblings had a tearful reunion by telephone. We were inseparable as children, Henry told his sister: "Grandma never told me she was giving you away."

Soon, Lai-sim created her own version of an extended family. First she added Henry, whom she persuaded to move to Ottawa, then she found him a wife in Hong Kong whom he sponsored as his bride. The extra helping hands proved a lifeline for Lai-sim and Yu-nam when he was confined to hospital for six months with tuberculosis. Lai-sim got the family on welfare. In order to keep up remittances to their families, she got a job under the table, washing dishes at the Ding Ho

Café. There, she put in twelve-hour shifts on nights that Henry had off from the kitchen at the Cathay House Restaurant, so that he could mind Billy for her.

Yet Lai-sim still had time to dream. On her walks in the neighbourhood, she watched a high-rise go up. If I had money, I'd like to own a building like that, she told herself. She passed by storefronts on Bank Street and imagined the premises as her own café. With her eye for opportunity, she spied a chance to become a homeowner when her grandfather retired to Ottawa. He took a room in a boarding house one street over, on Waverley. Lai-sim had the idea that she and Henry, whose wife, Chun, by then was expecting their second child, could afford to buy that very house. The smallest on the block, it was in the least desirable location, bordering Colonial Furniture's parking lot. She got Henry to talk to the landlord, a Jewish gentleman, who agreed to sell. Their grandfather loaned Lai-sim her share, and paid Henry's from his pending inheritance of the proceeds from the sale of the Altona café. With that, Lai-sim Yee became a homeowner, living a few steps from the woman she recognized from Frank Street.

"IF I'M NOT ON THIS SIDE, I'm on that side," Lai-sim Leung and Lui-sang Wong instructed their families, should anyone need one or the other and have to go looking for her.

"Or, if I'm not on that side, then I'm on this side."

Like two twittering birds on a wire, the women surveyed the landscape of their shared present, the newness of their lives in Canada. At their backs was China, from which they had escaped and could not, perhaps ever, return. The two friends did not bring up the past that was China. Everyone knows you can't have a good life in wartime. And that it was bad when the Communists came. To bring up the past would be to talk about it too much and not enough at the same time. Memories push up and then you have to push them back down.

THE ARREST OF See-fat Hum had been an ambush.

On the eve of the lunar new year of 1950, the Hum family unlocked all doors and opened all windows, to let go of the old year and welcome the new. Like everyone at the table, eight-year-old Lui-sang eagerly anticipated the traditional *fat choy* soup. The new year's greeting of *Kung hey fat choy!* bestows a wish of good fortune and prosperity while conjuring thoughts of the rich soup, laden with thin strands of black moss fungi, bean curd strips as fine as silk, pungent mushrooms, oysters and salted turnip.

Suddenly, two policemen, brandishing rifles, barged in. They hoisted See-fat out of his chair. "You are going to jail! You are an enemy of the People! You do bad things against the Revolution!" As they manhandled him out the door, Lui-sang wailed after her father, "*Baba!*" But her mother, Hoi-sui, declared that she was unafraid; she felt certain that the Communist Party cadres in charge would soon see their mistake and release her husband.

See-fat had been arrested because of his position as the village's financial administrator. Yet, he held that job at the behest of the villagers. In 1937, by order of the Nationalist government, the village lost its Kuomintang county administrators to the war effort against the Japanese. The people of the village asked See-fat's father if he'd consider giving up his son to the job, since he'd gone to a reputable military school and was the best-educated man in the village.

A week after his arrest, an aunt with contacts in the Communist Party brought dire news: See-fat was to be shot the next morning. She hastily added that she knew the route by which the police would lead See-fat out of the village. They could go there and watch for him to pass by, so that they could see each other's faces one last time.

Hoi-sui, stricken, said she could not bear to go. She was four months along in her pregnancy and feared the anxiety of the moment would cause her to miscarry.

The aunt spoke solemnly to Lui-sang, giving instructions for the morning. Where to go, where to stand. "Hang on to your little brother with one hand, and your little sister with the other, and wait for your father to come."

The next morning Lui-sang's younger siblings, one six and the other three, could not understand why they stood at the roadside. Finally, she saw their father, walking with his hands bound together behind his back. "*Baba!*" she called out. His eyes met hers, then he said, "Listen to your mama and look after your little brother and sister."

Back at home, Hoi-sui, who had remained behind with her youngest child, aged two, asked of Lui-sang, "You saw your father go away?" She nodded.

Yet no confirmation was ever delivered to Hoi-sui of her husband's death.

Life under the Communists grew more dangerous. In the south, the Party, seeking to carry out Mao's Land Reform campaign, classified households as rich households or poor households. The rich were labelled landlords and condemned as capitalists who exploited the poor. As obvious as protruding nails, the "rich" were sojourners who'd gone to Gold Mountain, and spent what they'd earned there to build a house, two even three stories high, and to buy land. Once admired, they were now vilified.

The Communists labelled the absent See-fat Hum as a landlord, and confiscated his family's farm and the store where they sold their farm products. "Where did you get the money?" they asked his wife. They answered the question themselves: "You took it from the People for yourselves!" Hoi-sui protested, telling them what they already knew— that their farming operation and their two-storey house were built with what See-fat's father had saved in his decades abroad, working at his brother's laundry in Halifax, Nova Scotia. The cadres did not stop with the family's business. A work team came to help themselves to the family's furniture and farm implements. When they removed the garden tools that Hoi-sui used to tend the plot beside the house, she was defiant: "What? I'm supposed to hoe my garden by hand? And how shall I do that?" The leader answered by striking her on the side of the head with his rifle butt. Next, the Communists confiscated the house, and the family joined other evicted families crammed together in idle storage and animal sheds in the village.

The cruelty visited on a neighbour, a sojourner's family like theirs but much wealthier, added to the family's anguish about See-fat's fate. They could more easily face the possibility of death by a bullet to the back of the head than a gruesome drawn-out death like that of their neighbour. The patriarch of that family, also surnamed Hum, presided over a large household that included young children who were Lui-sang's playmates. He'd fled ahead of the Communists back to Perth, Ontario. By the time the Communists had finished torturing his younger brother, his body was so broken and bloodied that his captors had to heave him into a basket and carry him on a shoulder pole to move him.

Three years passed before the well-connected aunt claimed to have found reliable information about the verdict in See-fat's case. She reported that a struggle session had been held against five prisoners, See-fat among them. The packed audience divided itself in half: on one side sat the poorest from their village, who sprang to their feet to denounce, assail and humiliate each prisoner in turn. On the other were those less poor, who knew enough to shout slogans and look enthusiastic but otherwise to keep their mouths shut. When the judges called for a verdict in each case, cries erupted of "Shoot him!" The judges confirmed the death sentence, and guards took the condemned outside, to be shot immediately. Last to face the crowd was See-fat. Each speaker began by repeating the familiar litany of accusations; but curiously, their pronouncements only obfuscated See-fat's crimes. Many spoke about how, as the village administrator, he had managed the community fish pond. The administrator's responsibility was to levy and collect annual fees from each family to purchase hatchlings for the pond, and at season's end, to decide the distribution of fish. But with the soaring inflation brought on by the war, families had seen their savings evaporate. Speaker after speaker, from both sides of the hall, rose to attest that See-fat never hesitated to ante up on behalf of the poor, and often delivered food parcels to them from his family's farm.

"The poor people saved your husband's life," said the aunt. "As long as they could see daylight through the windows, they were going to keep talking, until they knew it would be too dark to take him out to be killed."

See-fat received a sentence of life in prison.

THE ONLY *Mama* that Lai-sim had ever known told her the story of her adoption when she was a little girl. The story was embedded in her memory as if anchoring a beginning, so that life could continue, lovingly, in the middle.

"You were born in 1937, in the first year of the Resistance War. Your family, the Yees, were poor. They owned no land and had depended on money sent from a grandfather in Canada, a lifeline cut off by the war. Your mother, pregnant for the fourth time, gave birth to a boy. Within weeks, she and the baby had died of starvation. You were three at the time. Your father was widowed, so your grandmother was left to care for you, your brother, aged five, and your sister, aged six. But your grandmother suffered from failing eyesight and she worried about how she would care for all you children and keep you all fed. She decided to give one away. I gave your family a sack of rice and some sausages in return for you."

Lai-sim had a replacement mother but no father—he had died of smallpox before the war—two older brothers, also adopted, and paternal grandparents. Grandfather had been a sojourner, working abroad in a mine in Sault Ste. Marie, Ontario. He might have been there still had he not returned to mourn his son, only to end up trapped in China by the Resistance War.

As everybody did during the war, they lived with the ache of hunger, some days worse than others. Lai-sim saw that, but for a twist of fate, she could have been one of the girls that she and *Mama* would pass by on the way to market, an hour's walk away. Abandoned by their families, her age and younger, they wandered aimlessly, clothed in rags, dirty and barefoot. Some she saw fall, and she knew death was hovering. When the war ended eight years later, Grandfather, his savings long gone, wanted to use his head tax certificate to go to Canada to find work again, but on account of his advanced years Grandmother and *Mama* had refused to let him go.

The routine of Lai-sim's household remained unchanged. By day, the family gathered at her grandparents'. By night, as was common for a family short of space, its members slept separately. The house could accommodate only the two elders, as one corner was given over to the sow—the family's most important source of income—and another to chickens, kept in cages stacked high, behind walls that went halfway up to the peaked roof. *Mama* bunked in with adult relatives; the children slept together elsewhere, girls in one bed, boys in another.

Lai-sim had no thought that their household was in desperate straits. They had a small plot of land and a water buffalo to work it. However, she did know of relatives on *Mama*'s side poorer than them. When the twice-yearly rice crop came in, those relatives, who lived some distance away in another village, would show up to accept rice from *Mama*. They never lingered; Grandmother would yell at them: "Go home! You go home!" Afterward, she and *Mama* always had a vicious argument.

But once a year, on the day the sow's eight-week-old piglets were sold at market, such worry and strife were forgotten.

On one particular market day, Lai-sim awoke excited to meet *Mama* at her grandparents' house. She climbed out of bed and went outside to check the skies. Had it been raining, she would have been sorely disappointed. Market days were the first, fifth and tenth days of the month; if the weather today was bad, few people would bother to go. But the sun was out and *Mama* wouldn't have missed this chance to sell the piglets. This year, the pregnant sow had grown so fat that she and *Mama* had been certain it would have a large litter. Usually it bore as few as two; this year, it bore five. They would have made *Mama* a nice profit and to celebrate, as always, she would have bought Lai-sim a new dress.

Lai-sim skipped her way to fetch water from the well, her chore to perform at the beginning and end of every day. She then continued home to await her mother's arrival.

At the house, she found only her grandmother sitting quietly. "Isn't *Mama* here yet?"

"I don't know what's happening." Grandmother gestured toward the room that held the chickens. "Your mother has locked the door." She went to fetch a ladder, leaned it against the wall, looked over and yelled out: "*Ai-ya!* She did that!"

Lai-sim waited, perplexed, while Grandmother sent for a man in the village known for his strength. He was the local gravedigger and one of the few villagers who was never without work. He easily forced the door open.

Lai-sim peered through the doorway.

Her mother hung from a beam.

That afternoon, the gravedigger had her in the ground.

The next morning, Lai-sim, her face blotchy and swollen from crying, shrank into a corner of her grandparents' house as a noisy crowd of her mother's poor relations came to confront her grandmother. Why had there been no funeral? Why had the old lady buried the body so soon?

Grandmother stood Lai-sim and her two brothers in front of her. She jabbed a finger in the backs of the boys, so hard that they lurched forward. "Talk to them. You talk to them." Lai-sim began to sob hysterically.

"Don't hide behind the children!"

Sinister accusations rained down. The relatives had come in certainty that Grandmother had dispatched a warm body to the grave.

"She was still alive when you took her down!"

"Why did you let her die? You should have called a doctor!"

Grandmother stared down the crowd. "Get out of here. Go home."

For three years, Lai-sim endured the teasing of village boys. Like other children whose families had a water buffalo, she minded the beast to and from the meadow, ready to goad it with a stick or pull heavily on the rope around its neck if it strayed off the path into the rice paddy or bent to nibble at the tender new rice shoots along the way. At the point in the route at the base of a scrubby hill where tall sugar cane grasses waved in the breeze, the boys would yell out, "Lai-sim, there's your *Mama*!" Lai-sim never dared look, afraid she'd see her mother's restless spirit.

Mama's death, like a scuttling black cloud, heralded bad luck. The sow died. Then the chickens. Then came Liberation, when the Communists, in the name of Revolution, persecuted average families and impoverished them. Grandmother died. Lai-sim's brothers married, and Lai-sim and her aged grandfather were left to scrounge for whatever grew in the wild, the taste of rice only a memory.

THREE YEARS AFTER LIBERATION, a stranger showed up in the village looking for Lai-sim and her grandfather. The woman told them she had come to smuggle the fifteen-year-old girl to the border of the mainland with Hong Kong. Waiting for her on the other side, she said, would be a man named Kim Yee—her birth father.

"How will I know it is him?" Lai-sim asked the woman.

"He will be calling out your name."

After her mother's suicide, Lai-sim had been bothered by the thought that Grandmother had remained dry-eyed over the death. Perhaps her grandmother knew what was happening behind the wall of the chicken coop. She wondered, had her mother been terribly ill, maybe dying? She seemed to remember her feeling unwell—and that both women knew they could not afford the expense of a doctor.

The stranger's arrival in Lai-sim's life enticed out of her memory her mother's last words to her, spoken when the two bid good night before going off to separate relatives'. Lai-sim had put it out of mind; how could her mother's chatter compete with the anticipation of a new dress the next day?

"You have a grandmother and a father in Hong Kong," *Mama* had told her. "Someday, you will go to see them." Now, Lai-sim believed that on the eve of her death, *Mama* had been preparing her for a future without her, but not without family.

———

LUI-SANG KNEW THIS MUCH about her friend Lai-sim Leung: that she'd lost her mother when she was a young girl. They'd be talking about the usual, about mothers and babies, about where they might take the children. Her friend would suddenly, if briefly, well up, and but for the movement of her hand to wipe the tears away, it could go unnoticed. As much as Lui-sang missed her own mother in Hong Kong and worried about how her father was bearing up in prison, she had the grace to avoid mention of family that she had, that Lai-sim did not. These are things to keep silent about; you don't want to make your friend, or yourself, feel worse.

What Lai-sim had once done alone as a new mother, she and her friend Lui-sang now did together. In the summer and well into the warm days of fall, they would meet outside their homes, each with a baby carriage. Lai-sim's was for Billy, and a few years later, for Jim. Lui-sang's was for Harvey. Later, Howard and after him, Vincent.

They'd walk down Waverley to O'Connor, then up O'Connor to Sparks Street, where merchants had extended a summertime experiment begun in 1961 of closing the street to traffic to create an outdoor pedestrian mall, a first in Canada. Sometimes they walked farther, across Elgin, past the railway station and the famed Château Laurier, the castle-like hotel opposite, to the Byward Market. There, they loaded the baskets underneath the baby carriages with ears of fresh corn and a large cabbage, maybe a turnip or two, and a big, fatty chunk of pork to be rendered for use as cooking oil. On days they didn't need to go to the market and the weather was fine, they went up to Parliament Hill. There they'd lay out a blanket on the grass, and let their children play.

Harry Johnston, his wife, Mabel, and their
four daughters: Mary (back), and (front, left to right)
Lillian, Doris and Louise. Back row: George (a relation)
and Fred, Harry's son from his first wife.
Courtesy Linda Hum

THREE

OBSTACLES

"TELL HER SHE'D BETTER COME real quick."

When the receptionist at the business school told Doris Johnston that her mother had telephoned long distance from the hospital in Kingston, she feared something dire must have happened with her father's health.

Clearly, it couldn't wait until the end of the school week when she'd return to Perth. Most weeks, she remained in Ottawa attending her secretarial course until Friday, then took the train home to Perth, so she could help out at the family café over the weekend. Ever since complications from diabetes had sent her father to hospital, she'd included a visit with him in the weekend too.

Doris's younger sisters, Lil and Louise, were waiting for her at the café. A cousin would drive the three of them from Perth to Kingston. Doris's eldest sister, Mary, a nurse at the hospital, and their mother, Mabel, were already at Harry's bedside.

WHAT WITH THE DEMANDS of keeping Harry's Café running seven days a week, on top of school and jobs, Mabel Johnston and her four daughters had allowed themselves to think that Harry's bout of ill health was one crisis being attended to by someone else.

The year was 1940. Harry was sixty-four years old.

If he'd not considered the timing of his death, he knew where he wanted it to happen. He'd spent more of his life in Canada than in China, and yet regarded his family's stay abroad as temporary. Even having a debilitating accident hadn't blown him off course. The same held true for Mabel. She too expected that, one day, the two of them and the girls would leave it all behind and go back to China.

That would have surprised most of the townsfolk of Perth. Harry Johnston had been a resident since the turn of the century. He'd begun as a laundryman, sold out to a relative, Joe Fong, and in 1919 opened Harry's Café. For the past twenty-one years, the locals had been taking coffee at the counter there. Everyone knew the menu by heart: sandwiches, hot dogs, hamburgers, french fries, steaks. Even if they were coming in only to pick up a pouch of tobacco, they'd check out the specials of the day—sausages, fried liver and onions were big sellers—or the featured pie, usually raisin, apple or cherry, depending on what Mabel had decided to bake the night before.

The name Johnston worked to obscure Harry's connection to China. When Perth's Knox Presbyterian Church bestowed the surname to replace his own—Fong, it had been as if to say the church had put China behind him, that it had reset the counter of his history. On May 6, 1899, an item in the *Perth Courier* reported this renaming under the headline "From Celestials to Britons": six Chinese laundrymen in town had been naturalized and received Anglo-Saxon surnames. Three, related among themselves, were thereafter known as Hamilton; three others, also interrelated, as Johnston. As if offering evidence of the suitability of the six to live among the town folk, the item lauded their regular attendance at church and how rapidly they were learning English. It further cited the three Johnstons for having "volunteered the loss of their pigtails. . . . [Now] their shiny black hair is shingled in orthodox Canadian style."

Like every Chinese emigré of that era, Harry had left China wearing his hair in a queue (compulsory in China as a sign of subjugation to the Manchus), and had stepped ashore with it in Vancouver. Instead of staying on the west coast where the Chinese concentrated, he headed east to find work through relations or clansmen who'd gone before him, or to strike out on his own. Most everywhere, whites were quite happy to have the Chinese wash, dry and iron their laundry—laundering sheets was a particular drudgery, especially in winter. At some point, Harry was joined by his brother. The two migrated ever farther eastward, until the pretty town of Perth enticed Harry to settle. He had a small nest egg to invest in some property and a laundry. Had the news item in the *Courier* told the real story of Harry's pigtail, it would have explained that he'd been suffering recurring headaches, worse at night, brought on by years of white people pulling and yanking on his queue, or so he was convinced. One day, he'd had enough and got himself into the chair of the town barber, pointed to the queue and said, "Cut it off."

While the Hamiltons sold out and moved on (reportedly to Trois Rivières, Quebec), Harry stayed and eventually opened a café. Before exclusion shut the door, he brought out two male relatives, an adult son and his young brother-in-law. Then his young wife, Mabel, and their five-year-old daughter, Mary.

The names Harry chose for the three daughters who would be born in Perth suggested yet more attachment to this new land. Harry borrowed the name Doris from the daughter of the publisher of the *Perth Expositor,* Lillian from the wife of the milliner and Louise from the wife of the butcher.

As if attentive to their children's Canadian future, Harry and Mabel had welcomed the kindness of Lola and James Rowe, a couple in town who took it upon themselves to be the "Canadian parents" of their girls. Doris surmised that the Rowes had felt comfortable about approaching the Johnstons, the only Chinese family in town, because she'd befriended Earl, the Rowes' only child, in public school. She had seen the merciless and hurtful teasing inflicted by some boys who took advantage of his being a little slow (Mary explained that Earl had been born a "blue baby"). "Those boys are awful ignorant," Doris told Earl's parents. On Sundays, the Rowes would come by—they lived a fifteen-minute walk away—to collect the three younger Johnston girls for Sunday school, where Lola Rowe was a teacher. James worked at Wampole's, bottlers of the cod liver oil that stood handy in every family's home.

By all appearances, the soft-spoken proprietor of Harry's Café, a church-going man, and his wife, who lived with their daughters above their café, had their loyalties close at hand. But in Harry and Mabel Johnston's minds, it was China's soil that they longed to have again underfoot, and when their time came, to lie beneath.

"IF YOU CAN'T FIND anybody suitable, then put up a notice that I am looking for a 'replacement wife.'" Harry, then thirty-seven years old, had made it clear to his relatives in

China what he was looking for: "She has to be willing to come to Canada to work long hours in my business." Harry's brother and cousins labouring alongside him at his Perth laundry scoffed at his expectations: "Who the heck is going to be willing to work that hard!"

The year was 1912 when Harry learned he was a widower, that the wife he'd married and left behind in China to raise their son had died. When he arrived back in the village to mourn her and to remarry, his relatives produced seventeen-year-old Hum Gow-nui. A boisterous and handsome girl, Gow-nui had a solid, square build. Her first thought on meeting the older man that she'd been promised to was that one day she'd be the one left widowed; his son was older than she was.

After four years of life in China with Gow-nui, and the birth of a daughter, Harry prepared to return to Canada to tend to his laundry business. Rather than leave behind his wife and child as he'd done with his first wife, he intended to have his family join him. Gow-nui, anticipating the isolation abroad, proposed that he also take along the older of her two brothers. Harry balked. He'd already decided to bring his son to Canada and was reluctant to finance another ship passage and head tax payment. Gow-nui, not shy about speaking up, compared her husband's situation abroad with hers: besides any number of male cousins and a brother already there, he'd have his son; she, however, would have no adult relations. "If I'm to go, I need someone who belongs to me. I do not want be all on my own there."

Gow-nui's was a family that had experienced loss many times over. Of the sixteen children her mother had borne, only four survived. Two of those were daughters and married;

two were sons, both at home. The younger boy, Fuen, had just started school. The older, Sang, an industrious boy five years Gow-nui's junior, would make a good worker, she told her husband.

When Harry wavered, Gow-nui delivered an ultimatum: Take Sang or I won't go.

Harry relented. The Hum family, not wanting one of the last two sons to go abroad unmarried, arranged Sang's wedding on the eve of his departure. His teenaged bride was left behind to live with them. In 1921, about a year or so after Gow-nui's husband, his son and her brother had left for Canada, she and her daughter followed.

Gow-nui felt she was setting sail into an uncertain future. Quite apart from the yawning age difference between them, she considered that Harry had a weak constitution, his constantly cold hands a bad sign.

A MAN WHO SPOKE only when absolutely necessary, Harry often declared his position on family matters with only five words: "We're going back to China." It was as if the words were a constellation by which he took his bearings. If returning was not the family's destiny, it was the prevailing wind that sculpted the contours of their lives in Canada.

He and Mabel raised their girls with the intention of preparing them for life in China. Mabel wanted them to have some ability to read and write Chinese.

She regretted her own illiteracy, relying on Harry to read letters from home to her and to script write of reply. She couldn't read the Chinese newspapers from Toronto or Montreal that visitors passing through town left for him to read. Of her daughters, she had less concern about Mary, for whom Chinese was her first language. However, Mabel fretted about how to make sure the younger three received some education in Chinese culture. Had they lived in Ottawa, she and Harry would have sent the girls to the after-hours Chinese school at the Chinese Mission. The five Chinese families there had pooled their resources to hire a teacher. Mabel decided Harry should be the one to teach his daughters. He dutifully returned from a shopping trip to Montreal (it had a tiny Chinatown while Ottawa had none) with calligraphy brushes, ink cakes and a set of elementary readers.

Doris objected on behalf of the three girls: "We don't need to learn Chinese. What for? We live in Canada!"

"We're going back to China."

Living in Perth, it was entirely possible for the girls to go months on end without seeing another Chinese face, other than a male relative in town. Never mind that the girls had been targeted with racial slurs of "Chink" by the same boys who tormented Earl Rowe, Harry had an additional worry about his children: "I'm scared you'll forget you're Chinese."

To remedy that, in the late fall or early winter, once business slowed after the last of the cottagers on nearby lakes were gone, Harry did what every Chinese who either owned a car or could hire a taxi and driver was fond of doing: he took his wife and daughters to visit other Chinese families. Although he saw these visits as benefiting his daughters, he took such drives as much for Mabel, knowing that she longed to see Chinese faces and hear Chinese spoken. Harry took a circular route to towns where he knew people, toward Ottawa and through the Ottawa Valley, down along the St. Lawrence

River to Brockville, then back to Perth. He'd stop wherever he came across a Chinese-owned café. Occasionally, a visit turned up a surprise if they came across a bachelor in the kitchen with the surname Fong or Hum. "We're related!" they joked. Nonetheless, the trips always fell short of one goal; the moment they were out of sight of the adults, the younger generation reverted to English. Just as learning to read and write Chinese fell by the wayside, the girls' language skills rusted away.

If by visiting another family, Doris and her sisters were supposed to identify with some Chineseness, as far as she could tell, being Chinese had to do with not spending money. When she and her sisters campaigned for a bicycle, their father had responded predictably, "We're going back to China." Doris thought the same frugality must explain why the Sims, who were the most well-off Chinese family in the Ottawa area, crammed their family of nine children into the rooms above their Star Café in Hull and ate their daily meal off a roughly hewn picnic table. (Anyway, Doris still found a way to secure a two-wheeler; the Rowes offered her Earl's bicycle after he'd outgrown it.)

Food was a more clear divide. What Harry served downstairs to customers was not what Mabel cooked upstairs for the family. Upstairs, she cooked rice and a stir fry, for lunch and dinner, every day. Her *bok choy* and swiss chard came from the plot that Harry tended out back, land he rented from the Walkers, who owned the *Perth Courier*. Only Mary preferred the food upstairs; China, the country of her birth, had apparently lodged in her taste buds. Her sisters declared the daily diet of rice boring, but they couldn't get enough of the hamburgers and french fries downstairs. They did avoid one downstairs food: milk. They couldn't get it down. Many Chinese have not only a distaste for milk but an intolerance to lactose. In Perth, dairy products were the pride of local farmers; the town's branded "Perth" cheese was sold in Europe. And Mary, having trained to be a nurse, preached milk's nutritional benefits. She urged her sisters to take some from the café and drink it by the glass at least three or four times a day.

Doris learned to lean against the prevailing wind blowing backward to China, and her sisters fell in behind her. She decided she was not going to make room in her head for Chinese characters. Besides, she argued, she didn't have time for that, with having to work in the restaurant and do home-work from public school.

As a young child, Doris once asked her father why he didn't offer customers Chinese food on the menu. He laughed: "They'd be scared we were trying to poison them!" Doris knew Chinese food wouldn't make Canadians sick. Take Mary's friend, Nellie Cohen. Nellie, whose father was a junk dealer, liked to visit upstairs so that she could sneak a taste of Mrs. Johnston's stir-fried pork. Mary told her sisters that her friend couldn't have pork at home. Why not? they wondered. Because she's Jewish, Mary said.

IN 1919, NO LONGER A widower and married for a second time, Harry returned to find the local economy of Perth booming. He purchased a two-and-a-half-storey building on Gore Street, the town's main thoroughfare. The building had two storefronts on the ground floor, and living quarters above, where he could house his arriving family, leaving the attic space for any bachelor kitchen staff. Harry kept the tenant on one side of the commercial space, and took over the other. He had the words HARRY'S CAFE printed inside the window and he opened for business.

One of the first matters of personal business to take care of for his son and brother-in-law was to adopt English names. Harry's son tried June because it sounded closest to his Chinese name, but soon dropped it for Fred. His brother-in-law, Sang, took the name James, but it almost immediately gave way to a nickname, Jasper—after a hamlet near the St. Lawrence River, where he had seen a memorable hockey game involving the Perth team. Harry put Fred and Jasper to work in the kitchen, the only place for them since they didn't know a word of English. Similarly, when his wife arrived, she became Mabel and his daughter, Mary, names chosen perhaps by the ladies at church. Harry had wanted Mabel to work out front in the café, to speed her learning English. He promised to step in to interpret if needed, but shy about her ability, Mabel preferred to stay out of sight in the back. She washed dishes and, eventually, took over the daily baking.

As if a toss of dice had rolled in their favour, Mabel and Harry's family remained intact in Canada. Had his wife and daughter delayed coming by two years, they'd have been kept out by exclusion. As it was, their male relatives had to follow the more typical path of Chinese men who'd gone abroad: work to save money, save money to visit China, save enough to one day live under the same roof as their family. Jasper had a wife waiting for him there. Fred, however, was unmarried. After his own experience of living separated from his father for his entire childhood, he preferred to have a wife and family here. He went to Ottawa to scout out the possibilities of arranging a wife from one of the handful of Chinese families there, only to find that, like Harry and Mabel, parents were still raising young families. He returned dejected: "Every girl is too young."

Fred would make a couple of trips to China, where he married and had a daughter, before finally pulling up stakes in Canada and returning home. Early on, Harry had considered giving his son a share of Harry's Café, but ultimately decided he'd keep sole ownership. "Fred's too busy going back and forth to the village," he told Mabel.

Jasper would work a decade at the café, all the while remitting money to support his wife and younger brother at home. Then he made two visits over six years. Each time, he took a healthy sum to invest in *mau tin*, and by his second trip, would build a house with two separate staircases, one for his own family and, when he married, one for that of his younger brother, Fuen. After Jasper's first visit, his wife lost a baby in childbirth; on his second visit, his wife gave birth to a daughter.

The narrative that contained the lives of the sojourning man or family relied on a certain amount of luck to arrive at its desired end. On that score, of Harry and Mabel's fellow travellers, Jasper was the one to have the most luck on his side. When Harry's brother Peter was ailing with tuberculosis, Harry had pragmatic advice: "You better go home, get your wife to look after you." Peter agreed; better to be sick in China where expenses could be kept down. The next word Harry received came from Peter's son. He wrote that he'd gone to meet his father's steamship, only to hear from the ship's crew that his father had died during the crossing and been buried at sea: "I didn't know how I was going to tell *Mama*."

Harry also heard by letter that his only son, Fred, had been felled by "heatstroke." Mabel had to break the news to the girls, who'd been close to him. The younger three couldn't understand how someone could die of heatstroke. "Doesn't matter what the cause of death is," Mabel told her daughters. "People at home always say, 'Heatstroke killed them.'"

BY 1936, OF THE THREE male relations who'd come abroad with the Johnston family, only Jasper was in Perth, recently returned from a visit to his wife and younger brother in China. Harry and Mabel had three children aged thirteen and younger still living at home; Mary was enrolled in a year-long nursing program at Queen's University. Harry and Mabel continued to steer a course that would, they hoped, take the entire family back to China.

Then fate delivered a hit on their blindside. How else to explain what was a freak accident?

The day had begun like any other, if only because Harry clove to routine. Routine gave rigour to the handling of his financial affairs. In settling his accounts, he was especially punctual and Monday was the day he paid the tobacconist, Mr. Depuis. Harry turned west out of the door of the café and headed up Gore Street.

The tobacconist's shop was a block and a half up the street. On his way, Harry walked past A.V. McLean's Grocery, Flour and Feed store, past the barber shop, then, at the edge of the Little Tay River Bridge, the bakeshop, where passersby could look through the window and watch the doughnuts sizzling in oil. Past the bakeshop and over the bridge, the street began to climb a gradient, more pronounced if one's eye followed the rising line of rooftops and chimney stacks. Harry crossed the bridge and went into Mr. Depuis's shop.

Harry was alone that day. Normally, one or more of the girls accompanied him, combining his errand with their own, to deposit the money they'd earned working the front cash— less the tithe Harry insisted they pay to the church—into a savings account at the Royal Bank.

While Harry and Mr. Depuis were concluding their business, a salesman drove into Perth with a delivery for Hulbert's stationery store. He parked on Gore, uphill from Hulbert's, crossed the street and went into the stationery store.

Moments before Harry left the tobacconist's shop, another driver returned to his car parked in front of the salesman's, started it, reversed, and then pulled into traffic and drove away.

Afterward, the talk was that, had the salesman taken the precaution of turning his wheels into the curb, his car would not have rolled into the street. People speculated that he had left his car in neutral or neglected to engage the hand brake. And that the other driver, in backing up to pull out, had nudged the salesman's car just enough to start it rolling.

Some passersby noticed the car start to move and yelled out as it gathered speed. Harry, hearing people shout behind him, turned to look but didn't understand what the commotion was. He neither saw nor heard the driverless car, as it veered across the street. It finally came to a stop against the Tay Bakery, pinning Harry against the wall.

The surgeon in Perth tried to save as much as he could of Harry's crushed right leg. He amputated just above the knee. But on account of Harry's diabetes, the wound wouldn't heal. Finally, the hospital in Perth sent for the orthopaedic surgeon to come down from Ottawa. Dr. Armstrong removed more of Harry's leg, to the mid-thigh, and when further complications set in, he cut it off right at the pelvis.

The police came round to see Mabel to tell her that the salesman, on his first day on the job, didn't have insurance. People in Perth remarked on how Harry kept up his good humour: "He's not a complaining man." Mabel took note that in this trying time for the family, nobody stepped forward to help her and Jasper at the restaurant. Thinking about how generous Harry was, in donating money and food to help people in need or to civic campaigns, she felt a twinge of bitterness. "People will help their own kind, but they won't help me. They probably think 'Let the Chinese help themselves.'"

Before the accident, Mabel had been ever more insistent that Harry avoid heavy physical work. With one of his trouser legs folded up and pinned above the knee, it was clear she wouldn't have to nag him anymore.

TWO YEARS AFTER Harry's accident, Japan invaded China. In a matter of weeks, the war cut off civilian traffic across the Pacific. No one could send remittances to their relatives or relay them through middlemen; nor could they get word of their families. The only certainty was uncertainty. Harry and Mabel didn't know if any of their relatives at home were still among the living, if they should be optimistic or despairing, hopeful or grieving. This state of not knowing produced a kind of paralysis.

Finally, Harry and Mabel grimly assembled Doris, Lil and Louise.

"We'll have to wait out the war," Harry told them. "We can't go home. Not yet."

The girls jumped for joy. "We *want* to stay in Canada. We were born here!" Doris felt relieved at her father's pronouncement, almost glad of the Japanese invasion.

The way Harry managed the stairs in his building after the accident served as an apt metaphor for China's place in the narrative of his family. Going up or down, he took the stairs the same way: he placed his bottom on the first step, then either lifted or dropped himself from one to the next. So, if he was resting, which he had to often because of pain in his phantom foot and leg, it wasn't possible to tell in which direction he was headed.

As war dragged on, Harry and Mabel settled on hopefulness, though perhaps involuntarily, as if it were a twitching muscle with a stored memory.

MABEL SAT AT HER husband's bedside in the Kingston hospital, anxiously awaiting her daughters' arrival. Every time a member of her family got into a car, she couldn't help but imagine the worst.

Her husband's accident aside, she still felt the emotional trauma from having been in a car accident herself fifteen years earlier, in her first-ever car ride. Joe Fong, the laundryman, had bought a Model T, and offered to take Mabel and Louise, still a babe in arms, out for a spin. It was his first car and he lost control; the vehicle went off the road and overturned. They walked away from the accident, but from time to time, Mabel suffered severe stomach pains. She'd recently had some x-rays and the doctor came back puzzled at what he saw. "Your liver is flipped over!"

Mabel breathed easier when her daughters walked in the door.

Harry lasted a few days, enough time for a goodbye with his family.

"I've provided for you, Mabel. You'll have income to raise the family. I bought six properties for you."

"What properties, Harry? What am I going to do with them?" Mabel had paid no attention to what Harry owned other than their building, with their café on one side and their tenant, the T. Eaton Company, on the other. "I don't know anything, Harry. I don't know anything about money. I don't even know how much we need to live over in this country."

Indeed, Mabel had never handled cash—not in China, not in Canada. Anything she wanted to buy, she went next door to Eaton's catalogue store, and ordered it. Her daughters did the same. Whatever they wanted or needed—such as crutches for Harry—didn't have to be in the catalogue; the ladies would have the Eaton's buyer shop for them. They charged any purchases to the Johnstons' "account," or more precisely, deducted it from the monthly rent that Eaton's head office owed Harry Johnston for the lease of the space.

Harry explained that he had kept meticulous records of his financial and business affairs, both of the café and of the commercial properties he owned downtown. But he'd written every entry in Chinese. Yet again, his wife had reason to bewail her illiteracy.

"Save money from the good times to cover the bad times," Harry counselled Mabel. "Remember, business isn't good in the winter; people don't want to dine out when the weather is bad. By the month of May, when the weather is better, people come around again. The cottages open in July. Tourists start arriving, passing through town."

Mabel had always dreaded this day, when Harry would leave her. Their daughters began to bawl.

Harry seemed so terribly sad. "I don't want to go. I'm going to miss my girls." In the end, Harry Johnston's heart belonged not so much to China as to his family.

A LONG WHILE AFTER THEIR father's death, Doris and her sisters asked their mother about something that hadn't occurred to them before. If their father and Peter had been the only two sons, why were they referred to in Chinese as First Uncle and Fourth Uncle? What happened to Second Uncle and Third Uncle?

Mabel had no idea. She explained that she had come late into their father's life as his second wife, to replace the first, who had died. Their Uncle Fred was the son of First Wife.

All of this was news to them. They were mystified by something else: why didn't their father's son and brother or other men, who had lived like bachelors on their third floor, bring their wives with them to Canada? Or send for them? Why hadn't Uncle Jasper brought his wife and daughter here, so that they wouldn't have to live under the Japanese in China?

Mabel couldn't believe she had to state the obvious. "Because the Canadian government isn't letting any more Chinese in!"

Now Doris was entirely confused. She had always thought it had to do with money, that it was cheaper for husbands to keep a wife in China. When she was a little girl, that was the only talk she'd ever heard from men like her uncles. All such truths out of the mouths of bachelors hid the larger truth—that the government had decided those of Chinese origin or descent weren't worthy enough to call themselves Canadians.

Young women volunteering their stenographic skills for "Canadian Aid to China (1947)": (left to right) Lillian Johnston, unknown, Louise Fong Johnston, Margaret Joe, Mary Wong, Helen Kealey, Doris Yuen.

Courtesy Linda Hum

FOUR

OPPORTUNITY

A REGULAR AT HARRY'S CAFÉ, William Relyea, the office manager at the Perth Shoe Factory, chatted to Doris over his daily coffee at the counter. If she was interested, he had an opening in the office; she could put to use what she'd learned at the business school in Ottawa.

Doris had cut short her secretarial course when her father died. She'd done so without hesitation, clear in her mind that she wanted to be at her mother's side to help sort through Harry's affairs. Except for the day of his funeral, Harry's Café stayed open for business as before, and Jasper, as head cook, kept the menu as it had always been. Now almost a year later and soon time for the family to remove the black arm bands of mourning, Doris felt that she and her mother understood her father's dealings well enough to keep things on track. And with her own sacrifice, of coming back home to lend a hand, Lillian and Louise had been able to stay in school.

The Perth Shoe Factory was one of Perth's largest employers. Its two hundred operators normally produced seven hundred pairs of women's shoes a day. In the First World War, it had supplied army boots for the Canadian military, and now that Canada had followed Britain into war against Germany, it was gearing up to do the same again.

Doris asked Mabel's opinion about the office job. Mabel had originally advised her daughter to go to the business school in Ottawa, seeing as the family couldn't afford to send her to university. Mabel urged her to take the job. Quite apart from leaving Doris free to work nights and weekends at the café, the position would give them both a window into how employers run a business. Mabel had no idea what was a typical wage or what to do with a pay cheque. She still didn't quite understand how banks worked.

The wartime economy created a bonanza and not just for factories churning out military equipment. The war rapidly transformed Ottawa, once built on lumber fortunes and in the last century the centre of the timber trade in Canada, into a government town. Needing personnel to run its wartime programs, the government hired as quickly as people could apply. Lillian saw a chance to move to the city. She persuaded Louise to join her in sitting for the federal government's entrance examination for stenographers. Both easily passed. In Ottawa, the sisters rented rooms at the YWCA (its goal, it assured parents whose daughters had to live away from home, was "keeping our girls good") until they could find an apartment to share.

At the Perth Shoe Factory office, Doris became close friends with a co-worker her age. Eva Devlin's father had been the Children's Aid inspector responsible for orphans, then served a term as mayor and was now Perth's long-serving justice of the peace—a post Eva's older brother, Eric, would inherit. The Johnstons knew the Devlins best from years of seeing Eric come into the café for candy and hot dogs after school. When Eric graduated to ordering his first T-bone steak and made a choice of "well done," Jasper came out of the kitchen with his cleaver mid-air, and in broken English declared: "You no get well done, you get medium rare!"

Not long after Doris joined the office, Eva's mother died. By then, Eric had enlisted and gone overseas. The girls compared their common fate of keeping company with a surviving parent. Doris confided in Eva how attached she felt to Mabel: "If my mother went anywhere, if she left Perth, I'd have to go too." But neither Doris nor Eva talked about moving on. It was still possible to dream big in a small town. Eva, known as a tomboy, a girl who could skate as fast as any boy and play softball with the best of them, had ambitions: she was saving her money to take flying lessons and to buy a small airplane. One day, she told Doris, I'll take you up with me so that we can both see Perth from the air.

DORIS AND MABEL made regular shopping trips to Ottawa. Their routine took them mainly along Albert Street, along a two-block stretch on either side of Bank Street where a half dozen Chinese-run businesses conglomerated. Interspersed among white-owned establishments—a tire shop, print shop, paper company and the imposing Hunter Building, the first federal office building built by Public Works in Ottawa—were two grocers, a confectionery, a café and a couple of social clubs.

Their errands included a stop at the Colonial Coach Lines bus terminal to pick up shipments of Chinese foodstuffs for their own table that Mabel had ordered from Chinatowns in Toronto or Montreal. She rarely ordered from Vancouver because of the high freight charges. Next, the two stopped in at the Wongs'. Mr. Sue Wong ran the family store, the Yick Lung, out of the front room of their house, and had installed his wife and seven children in the first-floor back room and the attic. (Another tenant lived on the second floor.) At the Yick Lung, Mabel could purchase staples: rice, soya sauce, tea, preserved sausages and ginseng, sometimes fresh Chinese greens, which came by bus or train from Montreal.

The store posted no hours; Mr. and Mrs. Wong said that if someone wanted to buy, they were open. But equally important, the Wongs' store functioned as a community meeting place. Mrs. Wong rimmed the small front vestibule with chairs, providing a place where the local Chinese community, and in particular, its wives and mothers, could alight to visit and chat.

During the first half-century of the Chinese presence in Ottawa, the number of families in the city were very few. When Canada imposed exclusion in 1923, only six of some three hundred Chinese in Ottawa had either come with their wives or sent for them. The Canadian government had been uncompromising on the day that the law came into effect; as of July 1, any Chinese on board a boat destined for Vancouver or Victoria that was mid-ocean or even in port could not enter the country unless they either had already paid the head tax or held a Canadian birth certificate; anybody else, even a wife coming to join her husband, would be turned back. The six wives in Ottawa were very nearly five: Mrs. Shung Joe's boat docked in Vancouver just as the Exclusion Act took effect. Her husband drew on his good standing as a member of the Presbyterian Church and enlisted a church official to help plead their case. The head tax was duly paid and Mrs. Shung Joe was reunited with her husband.

The number of these pioneer wives did fall to five when the owner of the Wing On, who opened the first Chinese storefront on Albert Street in 1914, decided his wife would have an easier life in China. There were only four upon the death of Jack Hum's wife. Jack himself died a decade later, leaving behind their three teenaged sons. Two of the wives were married to the brothers Sue and Shing Wong, both grocers; the third to Shung Joe, the only one of the original patriarchs—all of whom had started in the laundry business—to remain in it; and the fourth, Joe Sim, the restaurateur in Hull.

The so-called social clubs were all-male domains. Women did not set foot in such clubs, where gambling and Johnny Walker Red Label were enjoyed in equal measure. Nor did children, except as messengers sent from the nearby Canton Inn. Their job was to get the attention of the bachelor men absorbed in their games of mahjong and dominoes and fan tan, to tell them that a dinner order someone had placed was ready. For a time, Doris and Mabel's excursions to Ottawa included taking a turn outside the entrances of the clubs with collection tins for war relief in China, a fundraising idea of the pioneer wives. Mabel approved: "Might as well get money from the gamblers going in; they're not going to have it coming out."

Wives needing to get out of the house considered church their only option. Some had been introduced to the religion and the institution of the church by Reverend Gordon Taylor, a Presbyterian minister who travelled around the Ottawa area to fill in for absent clergyman, and made a point of befriending Chinese laundry and café owners and the bachelors who worked for them. Originally from Edinburgh, the Reverend could speak Chinese without an accent and seemed to have a deep knowledge of Chinese history and culture. He claimed that everything he knew he'd learned from a Chinese man in Montreal who'd been a scholar in China but a laundryman here. The Chinese were of two minds about the Reverend: some thought him to be a great man because he'd brought them to the church and given them Christian names. Others saw him as a busybody who was rumoured to meet regularly with Prime Minister Mackenzie King. In his first term as prime minister, King had brought in exclusion.

Come Sunday, the wives donned their tailored dresses and hats—Mrs. Joe took pride in her stylish hats—and attended the services at Dominion United Church on Metcalfe Street or Knox Presbyterian Church on Elgin. That they understood or spoke little English—other than "Yes" and "No" and "Too much!"— proved no hindrance. One can readily participate at church simply by observing and following suit; you sit or stand or bow your head or pick up the hymn book when everyone else does.

At Mrs. Wong's, they were back comfortably in their ele- ment, speaking in their native Toisonese. The wives, often with their children in tow, made for the Yick Lung straight from church, knowing they'd find Mrs. Wong there, always on hand to mind the store. Whether to complain or commiserate, they could count on a sympathetic ear from the grocer's wife. Such compassion sprang perhaps from the wellspring of Mrs. Wong's trials as a mother living with heartache.

In 1920, her husband could finance only one head tax and passage for a family member to join him in Ottawa. Mrs. Wong had no choice but to leave behind their only child, a three-year- old girl. She solemnly promised the girl that one day she'd be back with her father, that they'd reclaim her from her grandparents and live again as a family. In Ottawa, Mrs. Wong, filled with longing for her daughter, would sit by the open window in the room that she shared with her husband above his uncle's Murray Street laundry, weeping at the sound of children at the nearby school. Years passed, during which time Mrs. Wong gave birth to six children. She was pregnant with the seventh when the family readied to return for good to China. They booked their boat passage for the fall, timing it for one month after her due date. That summer, Japan invaded China. The war cut off the family's communication with the daughter in China, and all chance of returning home anytime soon evaporated.

If the vestibule was occupied most often by the wives, it served equally as a sanctuary for a few aged bachelors who sat silently sipping tea and smoking a water pipe. Their prospects of outliving the war slipping away, they came to enjoy the atmosphere of family created by visiting wives and the Wong children. The youngest child might play underfoot, but the older Wong children would be helping out, from addressing envelopes in English to Chinese suppliers, to loading up a wagon, or if in winter, a toboggan, to make deliveries to laundrymen whose work left them no time to shop.

Luck interceded in 1942 to land another immigrant wife in Canada, who took up residence in Ottawa. The government invoked "special considerations" provided for under the Exclusion Act to admit a Chinese family of four as wartime refugees: William (Bill) and Ethel Poy and their children, Neville, aged seven, and Adrienne, aged three. As the threat loomed of a Japanese attack on Hong Kong, Mr. Poy had been one of the volunteer motorcyclists who relayed messages for the Allies between the colony and enemy territory on the mainland. High stakes middle-of-the night negotiations between the Allies and the Japanese, brokered by the Red Cross, to exchange Japanese prisoners for Allied nationals had given the Poy family their ticket out of Hong Kong. Bill Poy's life had already been one of action and upward mobility. Born in Australia to a Chinese man and a half-Chinese, half-Irish woman, he had been sent as a teenager back to his father's village in China, but within six months he made his own way to Hong Kong. Bill found success and fame there as an amateur jockey at the Happy Valley Racecourse.

Once settled in Ottawa, Mrs. Poy, as beautiful and elegant as her husband was debonair and dashing, made an occasional appearance at the Yick Lung to call on Mrs. Wong. But Ethel, dropped into a city with a tiny Chinese community, no Chinatown, no Chinese newspapers or books or movies, and mourning what the Japanese had destroyed of her life in colonial Hong Kong where she'd enjoyed a genteel social life, would never feel comfortable in her new home. The wives she joined in Ottawa were almost a generation older. They'd come out of rural China more than twenty years earlier. They spoke their coarse village dialect, not her refined Cantonese; they called whites *lo fan*, portraying them as pale ghosts, instead of the *si yuen*, the more polite term meaning *Western people* that was used by the educated class or those from the city. Her experience of war, if anything, alienated her from the women here. She kept to herself the terror of life under Japanese occupation. She didn't explain that the reason young Neville ducked for cover every time he saw an aircraft was that he'd been on the rooftop in Hong Kong and had watched the approach of the first Japanese bombers, thinking them to be the British Air Force on another practice run. Why draw attention to the family's good fortune, when their relatives, if alive, still had to live with the enemy?

Talk at Mrs. Wong's stayed within the confines of the familiar, of their lives in Ottawa. Of the six pioneer wives, two had first-born children whom they'd brought to Canada with them. One of the two was Thomas Hum, who took responsibility for his two brothers on the death of their last surviving parent. Nineteen at the time, Thomas took over their father's café. The other was Jack Sim, chosen by his father, Joe, to run the family business so that Jack's eight younger siblings could stay in school and, as was their father's plan, go on to university. Tall and broad-shouldered, with chiselled features, Jack looked like a Chinese movie star. His younger brothers would later dub him the Chinese James Dean.

The Chinese community buzzed with the success of one of their own. Clearly, Jack was clever. As his father had expected, his eldest son bettered him early on, with his command not only of English but of French as well, having graduated from high school in Hull where French was the language of instruction. He started with his father's Star Café, catering to Hull's working class. Then, seeing future patrons in the influx of civil servants in Ottawa, he opened the sophisticated Tea Gardens on Sparks Street, between the Mayfield ladies' dress shop and the Lord Thomas hair salon. Later, Jack would guess right that city folk, new to owning cars, would want to get away from the city, but not too far, and to someplace with a view; Bate Island, with the Remic Rapids wrapping round it, looked west, where the setting sun dropped spectacularly into the river. Jack leased land from the federal government under the bridge to the island, then designed a rustic building with walls of knotted pine, a nickelodeon and a dance floor. On weekend nights, young people crowded the parking lot of the El Rancho, standing around their cars, enjoying a menu favourite, the chow mein bun, brought by car hop girls in cowgirl outfits. Jack went on to open a fourth restaurant, and when the El Rancho later burned down, he built a new one on the island.

One day Doris and Mabel dropped into the Yick Lung and found Rosina, Jack Sim's wife, pouring her heart out to Mrs. Wong. She was sure that one of Jack's white waitresses had her eye on him: "He's probably running around on me and I can't do anything about it!" Years before, on the elder Sim's orders, Jack had made a trip to China to marry, but he'd come back as he'd left, a single man. Ordered back a second time, he returned a married man—with Rosina, who, under exclusion, was able to enter the country by virtue of a Canadian birth certificate. Born in Alberta, she'd been taken as a young child by her parents to their village in China.

Not unlike Ethel Poy, Rosina found it hard to find her footing in Ottawa. She would never learn much English. Among the first to marry into one of the pioneer families, she met few if any Chinese women her age. Rosina wasn't going to get much, if any, sympathy from her mother-in-law, who, in keeping with Chinese tradition, expected subservience from a daughter-in-law. During Mrs. Joe Sim's long life—she would live to one hundred and four—the taciturn woman would have little to say of her past in China except for one story: her wedding day. On the day her family carried her in a sedan chair to her new mother-in-law's house, she parted the curtain to get a glimpse of the man she'd been promised to. She felt dismay to see that he walked with a limp. It turned out that Joe Sim had sprained his ankle in a recent fall while horsing around with some boys on a rooftop. Yet when Mrs. Sim told the story, this fact mattered not; limp or no limp, she'd already passed the point of no return.

MABEL WANTED HER daughters to escape her fate in marriage. "I was so much younger than your father. In China a lot of that happened; older men marrying younger women. Then we end up afraid our husband is going to die soon. I want you to marry in the Canadian way. I want you to pick your own husbands. I had to take whatever marriage my parents made for me."

Mary chose her own husband. She wed Captain Dan Wong, whom she'd met on a trip to Montreal. Sent by the Kuomintang military to study abroad, he was introduced to Mary at a Chinese celebration in the city.

Mabel confessed to her unmarried daughters that she'd fended off propositions of marriage for them more than once. A preposterous one came from a woman who wanted to make a group deal: her three sons for Mabel's three daughters. A Mrs. Jang, from Woodstock, a town in the rich farmland of southern Ontario, was confident that Mrs. Johnston would find her sons an attractive package: one was a cook, one had joined the Canadian Air Force, and the third, with a diploma from the Ontario Agricultural College in Guelph, ran the family farm. To avoid offending the woman, Mabel replied that it would be bad luck to have siblings marrying siblings. Bad luck could strike both their families, she said.

While Mabel wanted her daughters to choose their own spouses, she nonetheless wanted them to confine their choices. "Be sure to choose someone Chinese, because that will make for a better marriage. If you choose a *lo fan* there will be too many differences between you." Similarly, Mabel advised her daughters to avoid anyone born of a mixed union, and thus, only partly Chinese. "People who are half and half don't have a good standing; not like our own kind."

More often, Chinese parents made it perfectly clear that intermarriage was taboo: "If you marry a *lo fan*, I will disown you." Or, "If you marry a *lo fan*, I will break both your legs."

Yet even on the west coast, marrying within the Chinese race posed a challenge. Exclusion was accomplishing what the head tax had failed to do—it was shrinking the Chinese presence in Canada. The declining number of Chinese in the country, who remained overwhelmingly male, exacerbated the shortage of women of marriageable age. The same held true in the United States. As a consequence, Chinese on both sides of the border went on wife-hunting trips to Vancouver and San Francisco in the west, and New York in the east. Anywhere outside of big cities, a Chinese family could be the only one in town. And, more often than not, the bachelors in town were relatives, and working for them.

Some well-meaning ladies from the church in Perth took it upon themselves to offer Doris advice. "Don't go for any of the boys that come to your restaurant. After they leave your restaurant, they go to the bars. You've got a good mother; listen to her and marry someone Chinese."

DORIS DID VISIT Ottawa on her own to see Lil and Louise, and more frequently once they had their own apartment. When they had lived at the YWCA, she rarely went, not only because she had nowhere to stay but because they couldn't afford to eat out; they were counting pennies just to buy meals at the cafeteria there. It had taken Lil and Louise several months to secure their own place. "It's already rented," they'd be told. With so many new employees joining the government, the market was tight. But they started noticing that when another prospective tenant arrived to view an apartment, someone who wasn't Chinese, that person would be shown the space. Finally, Lil and Louise met a Jewish man with a basement apartment he was happy to rent to them.

At work, Louise's boss urged her to put Fong back into her name, in front of Johnston. "Don't ever give up the Chinese part of your name," he told her. Doris shrugged off the name change. "I like Johnston," she said. "I was born with it; it's on my birth certificate." Her sisters, enjoying the wider circle of friends and colleagues in Ottawa, both Chinese and white, pestered her to leave the small town for the city. We can find you a steno job like ours, they told her.

Doris didn't dispute the attraction of benefits like medical insurance and a pension. And as long as she didn't marry—she wasn't sure if she even wanted to—she'd have job security; federal regulations required women to resign their positions when they married.

"You should get out of the shoe factory," Lil said.

"I'd miss buying shoes at a discount. I can get seconds there for two dollars."

"You can't spend your free time in the restaurant. What kind of social life is that."

"The customers are real nice. Some come every day."

"It's kids who come every day; you're selling candy and sodas to kids after school."

"Nobody likes the soda fountain anymore," Doris said. "They're full of gas. People like to buy soft drinks in a bottle."

What Doris didn't say was that she was proud of how she and her mother had coped after Harry's death. She saw her mother and herself as partners, not unlike men who ran businesses together. She'd been the one initially to acquaint herself with the investment properties that Mabel inherited. Generously, two gentlemen in Perth, both regulars at the café, one who worked at the Post Office and another at the Customs Office, patiently explained deeds and leases, tax bills and filings. "If ever you get stuck, just come to us," they told Doris.

Plus, she appreciated the security that life in a small town offered; people looked out for each other. And her mother had come a long way. For the sake of managing the café and the properties, Mabel worked hard at improving her English and developing business smarts. It didn't take long for Doris to see that of the two of them, her mother had the better head for handling money and investments.

IF DORIS DIDN'T LEAVE TOWN to seek the company of other Chinese, they came to her, always stopping in at Harry's Café when passing by Perth. Some came specifically to call on her. Charles Hum, the middle of the three orphaned Hum brothers, made the drive from Ottawa accompanied by some relations. They came to sound out Doris on the possibility of marriage between her and Charles.

These particular Hums were well set financially. Besides the Ontario Café, located on valuable real estate on the corner opposite the train station and the Château Laurier, Thomas had opened a second café, the Arcadia Grill with the attractive

Art Deco facade on Bank Street. The novelty of air condition-ing helped make the Arcadia hugely popular. Thomas assigned his brother Charles to be the soda manager there; their younger brother, Joe, still in school, lived in a room above the restaurant and helped out after school and on weekends.

I have a chance to marry into the Hums, Doris realized. At the shoe factory, marriage was often a topic of conversation. One day, the girls in the office told Doris about the woman she'd replaced. They spoke of how the bosses had decided to get rid of her because she was costing the company money; she kept getting everything wrong. Typing *blue shoes* instead of *black shoes* and vice versa, that sort of thing. "Her older sister's smart enough," Doris said. "Must be, to have married the high school principal's son."

Charles Hum was short; Doris envisaged a husband who'd be tall. Mabel advised her to keep her distance, suggesting there was a rumour of a history of tuberculosis in the family.

Another day, a carload of adults from the Soong family, origi-nally from Montreal, showed up on their way from a family event to their home in Almonte, a mill town on the Ottawa River. Doris, meeting the family for the first time, was impressed with how easygoing and friendly they were. And she was rather taken with two handsome and athletic-looking brothers among them. In particular, Tommy, the older and taller of the two.

As it happened, the younger of the Soong brothers, Howard, began to court Doris. She asked her mother's opinion of him. "Well, you like him, that's what matters. He's too skinny to suit me," said Mabel. When he proposed, Mabel was pleased for Doris. She had only one reservation: Howard liked to gamble. "Gamblers only think of themselves," she warned.

Christmas at the Way-nees. Sarah Way-nee (centre); Hin Lew
(jacket and tie); Sarah's four children (from left to right), Helen,
June, Alan and Douglas; Irene Joe (second from right); unknown.
Courtesy Hin Lew

FIVE

BETWEEN

WHEN HELEN ENROLLED AT her new high school, Lisgar Collegiate Institute, a grey stone, turreted building in downtown Ottawa, she decided to choose her own surname. All through school, her family name had been recorded at the whim of her teachers as Ling or Way or Nee.

Helen's father gave his name variously as Ling Way and as Ling Nee. He had no concern for how it was anglicized or spelled. When he'd first arrived in Ottawa two decades earlier, in 1921, and taken a room above a shoe store on Bank Street, the canvasser for the city directory listed him as Ling Way. It would have been lost on the canvasser to explain the Chinese convention of placing surnames first: that Ling was the surname; Way was the given name shared with his brothers. In fact, the directory listing omitted the other half of his given name, Nee, which was his alone.

Neighbours were equally confused about how to greet Helen's mother, born Sarah Randall, and addressed her as Mrs. Way or Mrs. Nee. The Lings lived in the Jewish quarter of the city, centred around Chapel Street, and straddling the neighbourhoods of Sandy Hill and Lowertown, east of Parliament Hill. That was where Sarah Ling had finally found a landlord willing to rent to her. Apart from the occasional French-speaking family, the neighbourhood remained a Jewish enclave.

Helen's older sister, June, and her younger brothers, Alan and Douglas, faced the same problem with their teachers, which led to the awkwardness of family members' having mismatched surnames. Only one recorded surname in the family did not change: that of baby David, on whose tombstone was carved *David Ling*.

When it came time to register at Lisgar, Helen wrote her surname as Way-nee. Knowingly or not, her use of a hyphen conveyed her feeling of living between the side of her that was "Canadian"—white—and the side that was Chinese.

AUNT EVA WAS THE ONLY member of the Randall family who remained on speaking terms with her sister, Sarah, after her marriage to Nee Ling. She'd insist to the teenaged Helen: "Your mother was a friendly, outgoing girl." To Helen, Aunt Eva seemed to be talking about a different person. She didn't know her mother to socialize with anybody. Not even coffee or tea with a neighbour. She wasn't sure if that was because her mother was a loner or because she was snubbed.

Her father was hardly home, except on Sundays. Nee served as head chef and baker on the household staff of a family prominent in the wholesale lumber business, the Bremners. Six days a week, he rose at dawn to take the streetcar to the Byward Market, hoping he was early enough to beat other cooks and café owners to the pick of produce, fish at Lapointe's and meat at Aubrey's. His day ended at ten at night, later on evenings when the Bremners entertained. Regardless of the hour, once off work, Nee made a beeline for the social clubs on Albert Street.

Alone with the household chores, Sarah had her hands full. By night, she slept with one ear to June, ready to race to her side if she heard the telltale thrashing or gurgling of the seizures to which her daughter was prone. Even if the night passed without incident, Sarah slept fitfully. When the weather turned cold, she had to get up an hour earlier to get the wood stove burning in the kitchen and stoke the coal furnace in the basement. Until Nee finally had the money to put down on a house, the trying task of finding a new apartment always fell to her. She'd moved the family three times, the first after they'd lost everything when embers in the wood stove in the grocery store caught fire and the entire building burned down.

For almost as long as Helen could remember, depression hovered over her mother. Nobody actually said so; she guessed as much because her mother sometimes took to her bed midday.

"I don't have the energy," Sarah would sigh. She said it in response to nothing in particular; it was as if she'd accepted that anything of interest in her life had already happened.

WHEN HELEN WAS old enough to beg a story about her parents' wedding day, her mother allowed that she and her father had been married in a church. She added ruefully, "There were no guests at our wedding." Helen's mother wouldn't acknowledge the existence of family on her side, apart from her sister Eva. The moment Sarah Randall announced her decision to marry Nee Ling, her widowed mother and all but one of her three sisters disowned her.

Sarah Randall and Nee Ling married in 1922. She was twenty-two, he was twenty-seven. She turned their first home, the couple of rooms above a confectionery store on the corner of Somerset and Russell, into their own cozy place. She did all the work herself, the plastering and painting, and the hanging of wallpaper and pictures.

Then, in the first year of their marriage, the couple suffered a tragedy. Soon after giving birth to David, Sarah had an attack of appendicitis. While she recovered in hospital from the appendectomy, Nee decided he'd surprise his wife: to welcome her home, he'd fatten up their baby.

In China, fat equalled prosperity.

To Chinese who'd come to Canada as children, milk loomed like the bogeyman of their earliest memories. Neville Poy dreaded the morning arrival of the glass bottles on the stoop of their row house where his family lived on Sussex Street. His mother, Ethel, pleased at the sight of the clotted cream pushing the paper cork above the lip of the bottle top, would extract the cream, and as if it were a dose of medicine, would feed it to her two young children. Knowing they turned up their noses at drinking milk by the glass, she made it the extra ingredient in her cooking, pouring it liberally even into baked Virginia ham.

To Nee's palate, milk had a repugnant taste and smell. However, when it came to his trade of French cuisine, milk, butter and cream were essential. If milk was good for a baby, Nee surmised that cream was better. He ended up rushing David to hospital. The baby's bloated stomach was pumped, but he did not survive. Sarah came home to an empty baby basinette.

Aunt Eva said her sister rallied after David's death, that she had become pregnant again almost immediately and felt fortunate when June was born. Then the baby started having seizures. Eva kept telling her sister that June had a congenital problem, that she was born mentally handicapped, that seizures were part of it. But Sarah didn't agree. "I blame myself," she'd always say. It had happened in winter. She had the baby in her arms and went to climb aboard the streetcar. She slipped on the ice and down they both went, June's head catching the side of the streetcar. The epileptic fits began soon afterward.

BY APPEARANCES ALONE, Sarah and Nee Ling made an odd pairing. As a rule, men are the taller of a couple; she had six or seven inches on him in her stocking feet. Not only was theirs an interracial marriage between a Chinese men and a non-Chinese woman, but even more unusual, Sarah's origins were English. The local Chinese often said, "French girls go for the Chinese." As they understood it, such a girl probably saw a relationship with a Chinese man as having decent odds for success, maybe better than if she threw her lot in with a French Canadian. Chinese men had a strong work ethic and were sure to be savers. And any with the ambition to start a laundry or a café always lived and worked on the premises, so she'd have a roof over her head.

Sarah Randall, the daughter of a lineman for the Ottawa Hydro and Electric Commission, had met Nee Ling at the Chinese Mission. She was one of the well-meaning women who volunteered to bring their evangelism to the "heathen" Chinese, beginning with teaching them English. An attractive blue-eyed brunette with an alabaster complexion, she had an artistic temperament. She liked to sketch, taught herself to play the piano, and sang in the church choir. The Mission was in the neighbourhood of her church, Dominion United, and a bakery she patronized. It was also close to the house where the Joes lived and ran their hand laundry, where once a week she dropped off and picked up the Randall family's sheets.

By the time Sarah met Nee Ling, he had joined the household staff of the wealthy Bremner family. Nee had worldly experience far broader than anyone Sarah might have imagined meeting. In 1908, Nee, aged fourteen and pining for adventure, ran away from his home in the central Chinese city of Nanjing and made it to Shanghai, where a captain in the navy took him on as a cabin boy. He worked his way up, and eventually became a chef for the navy. He had a repertoire of dishes from around the world, and particular skill in French cuisine, including the art of making *petits fours*, acquired during a lengthy deployment in Marseille. Nee had also picked up a smattering of foreign languages, including Japanese, French and English. In 1921, he jumped ship in Montreal. Within less than a year, Nee's evident talent landed him in the brief employ of J.R. Booth, head of one of Canada's richest families. A powerful lumber king of the Ottawa Valley, Booth supplied the wood to build Canada's Parliament buildings. J.R. had family and business connections with the Bremners, where Nee ended up, joining a staff that included a chauffeur, housekeeper, maid and gardener.

Contrary to what Mrs. Randall might have imagined, the family of her disowned daughter appeared more white than Chinese. To white people, the children born of Sarah and Nee were "half-breeds." To the Chinese, they were *ban min bao*— "half white bread." But it was not enough to apply the label. A judgment was called for. Did so-and-so look more white or more Chinese? The verdict on the Ling children was that they looked more white.

In the Ling household, English, not Chinese, was spoken. When Nee Ling first arrived in Ottawa, he'd gone to the Mission not for English lessons but to find others with whom he could practise Toisonese, which the Chinese here spoke. Attuned as he was to his native Shanghainese, he found Toisonese as strange as a foreign language. Although he would never learn to speak it, for a brief time, he enrolled his sons, Alan and Douglas— not June or Helen; he wasn't going to spend such money on a daughter—in after-hours Chinese school at the Mission, where they would learn the dialect.

On the family's table, usually the last place an immigrant surrenders his or her past, Sarah only ever set out knives and forks. Chopsticks were kept in the cutlery drawer, but they lay unused. On nights when Sarah cooked, she made shepherd's pie. If she put more effort into it, liver with tomato sauce and mashed potatoes. On the Sundays when the Bremners called Nee in to work, Helen would walk her siblings the several blocks to their mansion on Laurier Avenue. Nee would show his children what he was preparing for the family and their guests, typically roasted partridge or pheasant. Then he would sit them down at a table in the kitchen, and set out cake and ginger ale for each of them. Members of the Bremner family always came into the kitchen to say hello to the four children. At Christmastime, they sent over dolls for the girls and toy trucks for the boys. Throughout the year, they set aside gently used clothing for Mr. Ling to take home—once, a fur coat. As Sarah did with every item of clothing, she took apart the coat at the seams in order to get maximum use of the material, to re-make it into something else.

On the Sundays that Nee had to himself, the family spent the day together. In summer, he would hire a taxi for two hours to take them to a favourite recreational area for Ottawans, the government's Central Experimental Farm. The driver would go up and down Morningside Lane and Cow Lane, Ash Lane and Birch Lane. Nee would have the taxi wait while they visited an Englishman with whom he was acquainted, who lovingly tended a large garden plot.

On Sunday nights, if Nee was up for cooking, Sarah's spirits lifted. She'd park herself at the piano and play hymns, coaxing the children to sing along with her. Or she'd return to a sketch of a still life she'd started. In the kitchen, the chop-chop-chop of Nee's cleaver produced dinner. If by chance, on the previous Friday, a neighbour's child had knocked on the door—"Please, Mrs. Way, can you buy this chicken from my mother?"—then Nee turned what had been intended for someone's Sabbath dinner into what the family knew to be his favourite dish: steamed chicken with lily buds. When the table was cleared for dessert, he might bring out a fancy cake or a selection of elegant *petits fours* he'd made for a party at the Bremners that week. The occasion would be worthy of the good china kept in the glass-door cabinet. And tea, served in the silver tea set kept on display on the sideboard. After dinner, the whole family, Sarah looking smart in one of her good dresses, on which she'd pinned a shiny brooch, and wearing one of her good hats, took the streetcar downtown to attend the evening service at Dominion United Church. After the service, Helen and the children continued home by themselves; Nee settled in at one of the social clubs, one street over, for a night of gambling.

———

"RIGHT FOOT, June, start on your *right* foot."

Every day, the teachers at Osgoode Street School made Helen's sister walk up and down the hall for half an hour. Helen could hear them out there, trying to change her sister's left-handedness to right-handedness. She thought it odd that the school should worry less about June's obvious mental handicaps—she was incapable of carrying on the simplest conversation without repeating the same thing over and over—and more about which hand she used to pick up a pencil.

Having to watch out for her sister made school stressful for Helen. Her mother had waited until her younger daughter had also reached school age before enrolling June, thinking the two girls could be in the same grade together. But making it home after school was an ordeal. Boys would lie in ambush, their hands clenched around stones in summer—snowballs in winter—waiting for Helen and June to emerge from school. To Helen's surprise, they yelled "Chink" at them; she didn't think either of them looked Chinese in the least.

Helen had a vague memory from when she was perhaps five, of a prolonged absence of her father that had to do with China. Her understanding was that he'd gone to visit family he had left behind in Nanjing—his grandmother and a half-brother. That year, the Bremners, since they were taking their own extended trip to Europe, had given Nee the time off. More evidence of her father's Chinese origins arrived in the form of a parcel from Nee's grandmother. Sarah and Nee posed their four children in the mandarin-collared silk jackets she'd sent, including one for the baby. Over the years since, until the war halted boat traffic, if ever a letter came from Nee's family, he'd dash off to the Chinese embassy. He'd ask a cook he was friends with to ask a favour of a desk officer: to have the letter read to him and pen a reply, enclosing a remittance to supplement what his half-brother earned fixing bicycles.

Helen felt she could fend for herself against the torments of the boys, but they upset June terribly. The teacher, deciding the solution was to keep the boys waiting so long that they'd wander off, detained the girls for fifteen minutes after everyone else was dismissed. The problem took care of itself in third grade. The teachers told Helen that her sister's classmates found her recurring fits too upsetting, that the school could no longer have her as a student and that her parents would have to transfer June to a school for slow learners.

Relieved of responsibility for her sister, Helen hoped, finally, to make friends. She soon discovered friendship to be out of her reach. A girl who seemed a friend one day would turn her back the next. She overheard loud whispers and giggles among other girls: "Don't play with her. Her father will chop your head off with a big knife!"

So when a new Chinese student showed up midway through the year in her third-grade class, she was ecstatic. Joe Hum—the Chinese in town called him Little Joe to distinguish him from his brother, Charlie—at fourteen was old to be enrolling in grade three, but his height disguised his age. Helen was deeply disappointed when she discovered she and Joe couldn't communicate. He couldn't speak enough English and she couldn't speak Chinese. Born in Ottawa and sent back to his father's village in China for his schooling, Joe had been absent from Canada for ten years, long enough to have lost any English he once had. Like Rosina, Jack Sim's wife, he'd been able to re-enter Canada because he held a Canadian birth certificate. Just as Joe and Helen began to bridge the language divide, his teacher promoted him several grades, and by the end of the year he was transferred to another school.

Thereafter, Helen gravitated to another outcast like herself. Her ears caught other girls' talk in the halls and schoolyard about her friend, Ann Hutchins: "She doesn't have a father!" Ann's mother, a divorcee, was raising Ann and her sister on what she could make cleaning houses. Doesn't matter to me, Helen told herself.

IN 1941, FINDING HERSELF part of an entirely new student population at Lisgar Collegiate, Helen felt new eyes judging her. Although small in stature, she was striking, and when she flashed her brilliant smile, she stood out in a crowd of girls.

Helen noticed that from white boys among the "Canadian" students she couldn't even get a hello. She began to understand why, whether boys or girls, her only friends were Jewish, or half-Jewish; they knew what it was to be discriminated against. She appreciated that one Jewish boy faithfully walked home with her. Neither of them worried that anyone would report to their parents that they spent time together; the Chinese and Jews both believed in marrying their own kind. Helen couldn't help but make comparisons between her Jewish friends' families and her own. Quite casually, they invited her into their homes. Their furnishings were as simple as those of her own family, but they were not at all self-conscious about how they lived. Unlike her parents, theirs had some education. Their conversation kept coming back to saving for their children to go to university, hopefully McGill, if they had the marks to qualify under the university's quota limiting Jewish enrolment.

At Lisgar, the biggest change that Helen experienced was being in the company of Chinese students for the first time since she'd spent a few months in grade three with Joe Hum. Because the pioneer Chinese families' businesses, where they lived and worked, were downtown, their children had always been classmates. Those who were the same age were almost like family to each other, a cohort that had gone together through public school and the after-hours Chinese school at the Mission. As well, they had the same after-school and weekend obligations to help out at the family grocery store, laundry or café. In Helen's grade, the Chinese students numbered three: Joe Hum, whom she'd caught up with; Irene Joe, the second of seven children of the Joes who owned Joe's Laundry & Cleaners ("Cleaners" was added when dry cleaning came in); and Mabel Wong, the third eldest of the eight children whose family operated the Yick Lung store.

It was difficulty in her physics course that drew Helen into a closer friendship with these three Chinese students. Also finding physics a struggle, they formed a study group and Helen joined in. Such Chinese children could not generally expect help with school on the home front. Quite apart from having quickly surpassed their immigrant parents' level of education, they had a language gap at home, a combination of their fading ability in Chinese and their parents' limited English. As a consequence, the children would stumble for a word and struggle to express what they felt. The parents, in turn, would look on uncomprehending, their expressions misinterpreted as stoicism or aloofness. Parent and child were caught in a no man's land where much was lost in translation.

By the early 1940s, a growing number of the first generation of Ottawa-born Chinese had reached their teen years and were looking for fun outside their homes. Helen and her new Chinese friends passed time walking around Parliament Hill and posing for pictures by the statues. Joe Hum owned a camera, bought from saving what he earned working at his brothers' Arcadia Grill. In the winter of 1941, some teenaged boys who knew each other from Chinese school formed an exhibition hockey team called the Chinese Aces, to play games in and around Ottawa and raise funds for war relief in China. Some families supplied two sons, and one family, three. To fill out the roster, the team recruited half-Chinese boys; Helen's brother Alan played goal.

Helen's friends and other teenagers of Ottawa families were inspired to form a social group at the Mission to organize get-togethers for themselves. They founded the YPS, the Young People's Society, of which Joe Hum would be elected president, to organize dances and parties at the Mission. Come summer, they planned excursions such as picnics on the twenty-fourth of May, the holiday that marked the birthday of Queen Victoria, at Britannia Beach, where they roasted hot dogs and cooked hamburgers.

Coincidentally with these teens' coming of age, Ottawa had an influx of Chinese who had come to take government jobs. Helen's circle would widen. One evening, Joe Hum brought along a friend who was new in town. In 1942, universities across Canada had suspended graduate studies in the basic sciences in order to supply manpower for the government's secret war research. Through Gan Chu, a graduate of the University of British Columbia, the teenagers subsequently met Dick Pon, educated at the University of Alberta, and Hin Lew, who had not one but two degrees, from the University of British Columbia and the University of Toronto. The three were the first Chinese ever to be hired by the National Research Council. With tutoring from such scientists, those in Helen's study group came through their physics course with top marks.

While Helen might have seemed to lean more to her Chinese side with her Chinese friends, the reverse happened when she was with her white friends. Yet, she felt neither white enough nor Chinese enough to satisfy either group.

SARAH'S SISTER Eva married and moved with her new husband to a town over the border in New York State, sixty miles from Ottawa. Marriage added enough to the distance that her relationship with Sarah would gradually fade away. But coincidentally, after more than a decade of absence from Sarah's life, their mother had reappeared. Helen had imagined her grandmother to be a stern, formidable lady; she found her nothing of the sort, but a rather ordinary matronly woman.

Mrs. Randall's reconciliation with Sarah had less to do with her than with one of her other daughters. Marjorie had married a farmer in Uxbridge in southern Ontario. She had suffered a nervous breakdown, and Mrs. Randall was convinced that his drinking had been the cause. Marjorie was admitted to the Asylum for the Insane in Brockville, but her condition, even years later, never improved. What had most grieved Mrs. Randall was the thought of her six grandchildren being deprived of a mother.

The burden of Marjorie's plight fell on Mrs. Randall, who ended up raising five of her six grandchildren. The loneliness of it echoed her own struggle to raise four young daughters when she was left a widow. After Mr. Randall's death, she couldn't be home for her girls as much as she wanted because she had to find a way to support them. Fortunately, her husband's employer, Ottawa Hydro and Electric Commission, gave her a job cleaning their downtown head office. Of course, linemen knew their job to be highly dangerous and they took it at their own risk. But the company took pity on Mrs. Randall. Bad enough that her husband, a strapping tall man, was electrocuted, but he'd waited four hours to be rescued, while impaled on one of the pole's climbing rungs. He'd never had a chance, suffering for months in hospital before he succumbed.

"Your husband is the only decent son-in-law," Mrs. Randall told Sarah. She took it as faint praise. She believed her mother's change of heart had occurred only because the sins of one son-in-law now paled against those of another: being Chinese was not as bad as being a drunkard.

As is the nature of families, the layers of guilt and blame, remorse and regret become, in the end, fictions that torment. Nothing seemed to save Sarah Ling from a slow but determined retreat into herself. Perhaps she knew that, though life had not unfolded as expected, or as hoped, it still held possibility, because from time to time she'd suddenly blurt out: "Oh, I wish I could run away and leave the bunch of you!" In those moments, she showed a spark of life. Of course, she'd never do such a thing. How many times had Helen heard people say to her mother, "You should put June in a home"? She knew what her mother must have thought—that June already was home.

Jasper Hum at work at Harry's Café, Perth, Ontario.
Courtesy Linda Hum

SIX

FORTITUDE

WHAT ADVICE HAD he given her on his deathbed? "Save money from the good times to cover the bad times." But in the decade since the end of the war, the good times, brought on by an expanded public sector rolled on; the government needed workers to help prepare for the postwar economy. Canadians everywhere were enjoying growth and prosperity. Coming out of the war, Canada demonstrated that it had one of the strongest economies among Western nations. Canadians were working fewer hours and earning more, enjoying new social welfare benefits like family allowances and unemployment insurance. In this mood of new-found optimism, they began to have the families they'd postponed, starting a baby boom.

"The dollars are flying all over," said Mabel Johnston. She had taken advantage of her own stockpile of cash to renovate the interior of Harry's Café. She upgraded the countertop to a green linoleum, edged in chrome, re-covered the swivel seats in dark green vinyl and hung a huge mirror on the wall so that it reflected the shelves of coloured glassware for the soda fountain. And she added two jukeboxes, topping one with a slab of marble on which she could roll out the pastry for her pie crusts. But Mabel was proudest of two additions to the café: a built-in icebox and a telephone. She hired Perth's best carpenter to design and construct the icebox; he'd also worked on the addition to the town's Jergens soap factory. As for the telephone, she astutely predicted that boaters vacationing nearby would enjoy the convenience of phoning in their take-out orders of sandwiches and cold drinks for a day on the water. And, later, they could phone again to order dinner to take back to their cottages, to save themselves the bother of cooking.

Mabel couldn't have predicted, however, that the greatest benefit of the telephone was that it allowed her to keep tabs on her brother Jasper. She'd been able to follow him around for the four years after he'd left Harry's Café to work in various restaurants in the Ottawa Valley, including the Quebec side of the river. By the sound of his voice on the other end of the telephone, Mabel could tell if he was the Jasper she'd always known—someone who worked hard, who cared about others more than himself. Now that he had his own café, she wanted to believe that he'd stay focused. A year ago, he and several partners, including Doris's husband, Howard, had opened the Astor Café in Smiths Falls. Her brother had to hang on only a few more months, until the date Mabel circled on the calendar—October 19, 1957—when his family would arrive in Canada. Until that happened, however, Mabel intended to keep a watchful eye. In what seemed a lifetime ago, she had bargained with Harry to keep Jasper in her life; everything that happened afterward turned on that selfish decision.

She was glad of where she'd decided to install the phone, at the base of the stairs. There, it served the café and was also handy for those living above—now just her alone on the second floor and the kitchen staff on the top floor. When she got Jasper on the line, she liked nothing more than to park herself on the bottom step and chat away. Eventually, they'd have to ring off. "If I could do it over again, I'd learn to drive," Mabel would tell her brother. After all, Smiths Falls was only twelve miles away.

"EVERYTHING IS LOST; they took it all." That seemed the most that could be said.

People preferred to deal in silence with what was happening to family in China, now that the Communists, within months of taking power in October 1949, had imposed Land Reform on the south. If anything, others thought Jasper Hum ought to be thankful to have escaped with his life—unlike some other husbands who'd returned, Jasper hadn't waited around to see what the Communists had in store for him; luckily, he'd fled back to Canada.

From the first frightful news stories out of China, it had been apparent that in the province of Guangdong, the former stronghold of the Nationalists, Land Reform was one way for Communist Party cadres to exact revenge on fellow villagers with whom they'd had grievances or had envied. Sojourners like Jasper Hum, who'd invested their savings in houses and land in the village and come back to retire, were obvious targets.

"Lots of people have been killed; lots of people have been tortured." What more could people say?

Such talk, like a roadblock put up against feelings of helplessness, only upset Jasper more. His emotions had swung cruelly from elation to despair. When the Resistance

War ended in 1945, he'd been overjoyed to learn that his entire household had survived. He made the decision to pack up his life in Canada, ending a twenty-seven-year separation from his wife. Of course, men like him, able to come and go, had always to weigh the "right time" to be in either Canada or China. But whatever the future held under the Communists, no one in either country believed it could be worse than the atrocities and suffering endured during the Japanese occupation.

Jasper was not alone in his sentiments, nor in his decision to go home. Chong-sam Hum, one of the most prominent among the Hum clans in the Ottawa area (he could trace his clan back twenty-eight generations) followed suit. In 1947, a year after Jasper left for China, the well-liked restaurateur in Ottawa sold his Sun Café and moved back to China. But in what would make a fateful difference, Chong-sam had thought to register with Canadian Immigration a wife and two sons who lived in China, even though he had no intention of ever returning with them to Canada.

Jasper had returned triumphantly to his village. By the grace of Harry's Café, hard work and a Spartan life abroad, he was one of the wealthiest villagers. He moved back into the comfortable house he'd built for his family and that of his now-married brother, Fuen. He owned more than enough *mau tin* to support both, allowing him to rent out parcels to other villagers. He also established a clinic and herbal dispensary for Fuen, whose education as a doctor of Chinese medicine brought distinction to the family. Jasper had only one unfulfilled duty to his ancestors: he had a daughter—now a teenager—but no son. In short order, Fuen and his wife took care of that obligation. Already parents of a young daughter, they produced two sons in quick succession. Fuen gave the younger one in name to his brother.

Then came the swing to despair. Suddenly, the civil war turned in favour of the Communists. In early 1949, as their soldiers advanced on the south, Chong-sam's wife, Loo-shee, declared to her husband, "There's no future for us here." At her urging, he went back to Canada, planning, once there, to sponsor her and their two sons.

Jasper lingered as long as he dared. He would have liked to stay two months longer, as his wife was expecting their second child. But finally, in early 1950, he fled. He insisted that Fuen come with him to Hong Kong. Although the house, the land and the clinic were in Jasper's name, he worried that the Communists might mistake Fuen as the owner. "Don't go back until you're sure it's safe," Jasper told his brother. He had only one worry about Fuen: his predilection for opium. If he gave in to it, reason would desert him.

Back in Canada, the more Jasper heard about the Communists' retribution against sojourners' families, the more he feared for the safety of his household there. Yet, going on a year since his return, he had not heard a word from his brother, not even of his whereabouts. Jasper didn't know what to think, if his brother was being irresponsible, or if he should read something more sinister into the silence. Perhaps the Communists had intercepted his family's outgoing mail. In his anxiety, Jasper found it impossible, spending his days in front of the hot grill at Harry's Café while living on the third floor above, to carry on life as normal. He pondered going back to find out for himself the fate of his family, but some of the overseas bachelors responded in disbelief: "What, are you crazy? What, go to get arrested? Or killed?"

A VILLAGER COULD NOT BE faulted for choosing the familiarity of his home over the British colony of Hong Kong. Even Loo-shee, Chong-sam's wife, was drawn irresistibly by tradition. While waiting to hear from her husband back in Canada, she too had relocated to Hong Kong with their two sons. Although she took comfort in the knowledge that people for villages around regarded her highly as the district high school teacher, she'd worried that the family's three-storey house might attract the Communists' attention. But then, she felt the need to return to stand in for her husband at the reburial of his grandmother's bones, after they'd been exhumed, cleaned and placed in an urn. On the eve of the ceremony, two villagers, now ranking Communist Party cadres, showed up to whisper a warning: "Tomorrow, the Party is going to come to ask you to donate lots of money to the People. You better get out, now!" By dawn, she and her sons were safe again in Hong Kong.

Jasper's worst fears about Fuen's vulnerability were borne out. His brother had left Hong Kong and returned to the village for opium, an indulgence—possibly an addiction—for him that could not legally be satisfied in Hong Kong. The British, after regaining control of the colony after 1945, had declared opium a dangerous drug and subsequently banned its sale.

Fuen walked right into danger. Party cadres charged with classifying the peasant households in Jasper Hum's village labelled his as that of a rich landlord. When the cadres arrested his brother, they demanded that he turn over the Hum household's gold. When he denied the family had any, they accused him of hiding it. The more he protested, the more ghastly was his torture. His captors cut off his ears, then they broke his hands, then his feet. A few days later, Fuen died of his injuries, spared the knowledge of the even more gruesome cruelty inflicted on his wife and his sister-in-law, Jasper's wife.

Cadres in the village subsequently confiscated Jasper Hum's house, land and clinic, and banished the evicted wives and their children to a windowless, empty shed on their property. The men charged with administering punishment to the two women rounded up the two wives and their four children: Jasper's daughter, Ling, not quite two (the eldest, a teenager, was away at school in the north of the province); and Fuen's three: Shui-dan, Hee-jeung and Haw-wong, aged seven, five and four. Forcing the children to watch, they bound their mothers at the ankles, strung them upside down, and took a burning torch, dipped in fat, to their feet and legs. The men showed no compassion, the better to demonstrate they were not obstructing the Land Reform campaign.

After the torturers cut down the women, they tossed them back into the shed; severely burned, they lay moaning and immobile on the dirt floor. The children were left to fend for themselves. At night, the eldest, Shui-dan, trying to keep the other children and their mothers alive, crept out of the shed to scrounge for food and fetch water from the river. Any villagers who offered help would be inviting their own persecution; yet one family, that of the former village administrator who had also been arrested, dared to do so. Sent by her mother, ten-year old Lui-sang Hum showed up nightly with boiled water to be used, she said, to clean the two women's burn wounds. From time to time, she brought food, enough for a mouthful for each of the six.

Slowly the two women regained their health.

Four months into the family's confinement, the cadres released them from captivity. Later that day, Fuen's wife walked up the mountain, to the edge of a lake, and threw herself in.

MABEL HAD BEEN AS shaken as Jasper when, finally, a letter came from his wife with news that a year earlier, his brother had died at the hands of the Communists, that his sister-in-law had killed herself, and that everything that he'd spent his life abroad working for was lost. Mabel tried to be consoling: "You and I would have been the first to be killed if we were there. They would have tried to take what was ours away, and we would have fought them and they would have killed us. We worked so hard for our money. We had to live through so much to earn it."

For a time, Mabel tolerated her brother's despondency. But when he started hanging out with the poker players in the back of one of the shops in Perth, or took off with Howard, Doris's husband, for a night of gambling and drinking at the social clubs in Ottawa, she decided her brother was in a dangerous tailspin. Mustering the authority of an older sister, Mabel let Jasper have it. She told him he'd moped long enough, that while once he'd been industrious and conscientious, he had turned lazy and uncaring. She ended with a stern rebuke: "Get back on your feet! You still have a family to worry about."

Mabel held out the example of their clansman, Chong-sam Hum, who had re-established himself in Ottawa, reunited his entire family and prepared to start over. Sensing the growing popularity of Chinese cuisine, he had got right back into the restaurant business with the Ding Ho and later, the Ho Ho, both on Albert Street. He'd partnered with two savvy Chinese entrepreneurs in Ottawa: Thomas Hum, the son of the pioneer Hum family and descended from the same ancestral village; and Bill Poy, whose family had been admitted as wartime refugees and who'd been a regular at the Sun Café. Thomas and Bill had formed Allied Trading, an import–export company that dealt in goods ranging from fabric and clothing to televisions and polystyrene plastic.

Rousing himself to begin anew, Jasper plotted with his sister how to reassemble the remnants of his household in Canada. He had to first get himself naturalized. And he had to get the family out of his village to Hong Kong, the port of exit. All easy compared to the problem of how to support them once they arrived here.

Jasper wanted to open his own café, which was impossible without partners. But a cook who'd only worked in his family-run business and in a small town wouldn't attract investors like Tom Hum and Bill Poy. They were out of his league: Tom Hum drove a Chrysler, smoked cigars and had a riverfront home with a swimming pool, and a cottage on Meech Lake; Bill Poy drove a Studebaker, lived on picturesque Mountain Road in Aylmer on the Quebec side and owned a cottage on McGregor Lake. Both men had business and social connections outside the Chinese community.

Mabel and Jasper mapped out what he had to do. He'd have to leave Perth to gain experience in other cafés. And stay with the small towns. Life in such close quarters would force him to improve his English; in a big city like Ottawa, one could get by with Chinese only. Plus, he'd be able to keep his eyes and ears open for another small-town café that might be for sale, or a town with room for a second restaurant, and for potential partners willing to invest their sweat in a business.

Then came the matter of Fuen's orphaned children. Jasper's plan was to pass off the three young children as his own, as long as he could obscure their ages to credibly claim that in three years at home he'd fathered four children. Sadly, he decided it was impossible to say that Shui-dan, the brave girl who had almost single-handedly kept the family alive, was his. He sent word to his wife in China, asking her to break the news to his niece that he could not include her in his application.

More than four years from the date Jasper first began the process, his wife and the remaining three children—his own daughter, Ling, and Fuen's two sons—made it to Hong Kong for their interview with Canadian Immigration officials. All were approved subject to passing their medical tests. On that score, officials rejected the younger of the two boys, the one originally given in name by Fuen to his brother, determining that he displayed symptoms of autism.

ON A SATURDAY NIGHT in October, 1957, Jasper waited until the last customer left the Astor Café, then upended the chairs and swept the floor, making a head start on the day ahead. At three in the morning, one of his partners, George Fong, drove him to Ottawa. Jasper had never learned to drive either.

Five hours earlier, at ten in the evening, Margaret Hum and two children, Kenny Hum, aged nine, and Linda Hum, aged seven—the names they would later take in Canada—drew stares as the only Chinese among the passengers arriving at Ottawa Airport. Linda and Kenny themselves were wide-eyed.

Awed by how tall and white Canadian people looked, they were shocked when the men and women began to throw their arms around each other and kiss. "*Mama,* what are they doing?" asked Linda. Such public intimacy was unseen in China.

Margaret piled herself and the children into a taxi. Outside the Cathay House restaurant, the designated meeting place, she had to negotiate the children around inebriated men who'd stumbled out of nearby bars. Inside, they found the cook from their village who was expecting them.

At four in the morning, Jasper came through the door. He cried hardest when for the first time, he looked into the face of his daughter, Linda. The young girl could not take her eyes off the man whom she understood to be her *Baba.* All she knew about him was what her mother had said: that he loved to cook, that he'd doted on her two male cousins when he was in the village.

The sun had not yet risen over the horizon when the family arrived in Smiths Falls. George Fong turned off the wide main street onto Aberdeen Street, coming to a stop in front of the house that Jasper had rented for his family. He deposited his wife and the children there and shortly afterward left to open the café for the day.

Mid-morning, a neighbour, one of two spinsters who shared the house next to Jasper's, knocked at the door. They held out a large cellophane-wrapped fruit basket to Margaret. To show her manners, she nudged the basket back. The neighbour extended it again. The basket passed back and forth between them, one woman speaking only English, the other only Chinese. Finally, judging she'd shown an appropriate degree of unworthiness, Margaret accepted it.

———

LINDA WAS A TEENAGER before she brought up with her mother their ordeal at the hands of the Communists. She had previously broached the subject of what had happened with her stepbrother, Kenny. He insisted that he remembered nothing. He doesn't want to remember, Linda told herself.

Mother and daughter picked through the shards of memory.

Though she was only two at the time, Linda could clearly remember clinging to the legs of her cousin, Shui-dan.

"I can still see you and Auntie, tied up and hanging upside down. There are three or four men. They dip something in a flame and burn you, starting at your feet."

"I wanted to close my eyes but they said they'd kill you if we turned our heads away or if we didn't stop crying," Linda told her mother. "I can't forget your screaming. I remember that they came back and did it again. I remember that in the shed, you and Auntie couldn't move."

Margaret showed her daughter the burn scars that reached to her navel.

"Don't ever forget Shui-dan," Margaret said of the girl left behind in China.

Of course, Linda never would. Life got better for them after the Land Reform campaign ended and the Communists again allowed remittances from relatives overseas. In the two years before the rest of the household left for Hong Kong, the cousins had a happy time playing together, climbing trees and playing tag. "Shui-dan was such a tomboy; she wasn't scared of anything!"

Margaret continued, giving what would be the last word.

"On the day the Communists released us, your Auntie

said she was going to the market. She said she couldn't wait to see good food. She never came back. When I found out that she had gone up into the mountains and drowned herself, I thought, 'If only I was stronger, I would kill myself.' Then I thought, 'I can't, I have four children to raise.' I looked at you, you were so young. I couldn't leave you."

THE PEOPLE OF Smiths Falls could not have guessed that this reunited Chinese family had survived a terrible past, defined by separation, cruelty and death. They did not know that Margaret Hum suffered constant pain and discomfort from her burn scars, and recurrent infections in her legs and abdomen.

Her neighbours, the two spinsters, might have noticed that she loved to wear pretty dresses. They might have thought it strange that even in summer she covered her legs in opaque leotards. But they made no comment; they did not share a language. Their conversations were in the exchange of what went over the fence from their gardens, rhubarb and asparagus in one direction, *bok choy* and lettuce in the other.

Only one visitor knew more. Lui-sang Hum, whose family had been neighbours of the Hums in the village, had come from China the year after them. When she found out that the children she had once played with were living in Smiths Falls, she had someone drive her from Ottawa to pay a visit one Sunday. (It was her day off from her job at the New Astor Café, owned by an Ottawa branch of the Hums. They had added the "New" to distinguish it from the café owned by Jasper Hum in Smiths Falls.) Of course, she made no mention of the horror of the shed, and neither did they.

Tsan Wong in Exeter, Ontario.
Courtesy Tsan Wong

SEVEN

AMBITION

TSAN WONG FOUND IT A particular challenge to fix in his mind the name of the Blue Funnel steamship that had brought his paper father from China to Canada. All the ships of the line had Greek names like *Philoctetes* and *Protesilaus*. He wouldn't err on the date that his paper father had last visited China, however, as that was easy to calculate by when he had fathered his son, Wong Wing-ham, born eighteen years ago, in 1938. In front of Canadian Immigration officials, Tsan would have to shave three years off his real age. At least, he told himself, my paper father and I have the same surname.

If all went well, Tsan would live in London, Ontario, with Fourth Uncle, who'd bought the paper for him to go to Canada. Tsan studied diligently. He memorized the paper family's lineage. He assembled the details of their village to recreate it in his mind: number of rows of houses, location of the fish pond, names of neighbours on all sides; which direction the house faced; what each room was used for; who slept where. On it went.

In December 1955, when Tsan passed the interview with Canadian Immigration in Hong Kong, he sent a one-word telegram to Fourth Uncle: OKAY. That was the signal to send money for the airfare.

"YOU'RE GOING TO CANADA?" Tsan's colleague in the apprenticeship program at the British-owned Taikoo Dockyard could not hide his surprise. "What are you going to do there?"

"I don't know. Maybe work in a laundry, maybe a restaurant."

A cheerful youth with a broad smile, Tsan allowed that going to Canada had not been his idea. He explained that a brother of his grandfather on his father's side lived in Canada and had sent for him. His suspicion was that this was his mother's doing, that she'd written to Fourth Uncle asking him to find a way to get her son to Canada, not the other way around.

When his mother broke the news to him, Tsan was dismayed. He didn't want to give up his job as a machinist in Hong Kong. On his own initiative, he had applied for the same five-year apprenticeship program in which his older brother was already enrolled. Two years in, unlike his brother, he'd kept his marks above eighty-five percent, the threshold of eligibility to work for the parent company in England. With that goal in mind, he had been using a beginner's phrase book to learn English, matching up phrases like *Chee saw hai bin do ah*, when one wanted to use the facilities, with "Where is the WC?"

He wanted to refuse Fourth Uncle, but his mother insisted he could not. A widow, she worked at the shipyard as well, sweeping floors and collecting garbage. Tsan's job, while secure, was poorly paid. Everywhere in the colony, times were tough; disquiet about low wages, long working hours and overcrowded living conditions had spilled into frightening, large-scale riots. "Go, go," Tsan's mother told him. "You can get rich faster there than here."

UNTIL TSAN WONG HEARD from Fourth Uncle, Canada had passed only fleetingly through the orbit of his life, when he was a young boy. His adoptive father, Old Hum, a landowner and prosperous grain dealer, had been grooming him to take over the family business. One day, Old Hum brought out a dusty ledger, a record of money owed him from loans he'd made to bachelor men in Canada over the three decades when he himself had lived there. Now in his seventies, he had left for Canada before the turn of the century and made his way to Montreal, where he opened one of the city's first hand laundries. The arrival of Chinese men like him coincided with a spike in Irish and Jewish immigrants, each profiting by offering separate services to an emerging white middle class. The ledger showed that the amounts outstanding were substantial: fifty dollars here and there, even one hundred dollars. "Someday," Old Hum told the boy, "you can get that money back."

A series of misfortunes in Tsan's birth family had landed him in the household of Old Hum and his wife. When war came to China, Tsan's father and mother, with three young children in tow, had joined the tide of villagers from Guangdong province pouring into the colony of Hong Kong. In 1941, facing the threat of a Japanese attack, the government of the colony required all refugees who'd taken up residence there to prove that they had six months' provisions to sustain themselves. If not, they would be forced to return to China. Tsan's father fell ill and died, leaving his widow no choice but to leave the colony and return to their village.

Back home, the destitute widow saw only one way to keep herself and her two sons and a daughter from starvation: she would have to give up one of them. A fellow villager put her in contact with Old Hum, who was known to have extensive holdings, and to whom many tenant farmers in and around her own village paid rent. As it happened, Hum was looking to adopt a son, a boy who would be his protegé in the family's business. The Hums were not without sons of their own, but three of four sons had died young, before marrying. Old Hum judged the surviving son, though married with children, unreliable because he was addled by an opium habit.

The widow decided to give away the younger of her sons, six-year-old Tsan, because she considered him the brighter of the two. Unbeknownst to the boy as he set out with his mother on a six-hour walk to the Hums' village, he would not be making the return trip with her.

Mother and son arrived at the Hums' compound and found it dominated by a large two-storey house, with the usual fish-farming pond in front, surrounded by several outbuildings. The adults exchanged greetings and sent Tsan off to explore the fish pond. He amused himself by watching for carp to break the surface of the shallow water. Finally, having lost interest, he wandered up to the house only to discover his mother gone. In tears, he returned to the pond. Evening fell, but he could not be pried from the water's edge. One of the manservants from the household came to console him: "Don't cry, don't cry. Your home is here now."

Although slated to be the one who would protect the elderly couple's wealth, young Tsan received no favoured treatment. The family instructed the boy to address Old Hum as *Bak* and his wife as *Poh*—as elders rather than parents. He shared a room not with children but rather with a woman, a relation of *Poh*'s, whose husband was in Canada and whose remittances had been cut off by the war. At mealtimes, the Hums placed him at the opposite end of the table with the servants. Like them, he waited silently until the Hum family had finished their meal, at which point the servants could have what was left. By then, not a morsel of meat could be found among the vegetables. Other children in the household had *amahs* to look after them; Tsan was left to himself. The others had no household duties; before school, late in the afternoon, and again in the evening, Tsan was expected to walk·the family's water buffalo to and from the grazing grounds.

Increasingly, Tsan felt that the family regarded him as nothing more than a boy servant. At least Old Hum had enrolled him in school, which he looked forward to daily. However, the ongoing war could collapse the routine of daily life at a moment's notice. If and when the village head got warning of the Japanese army in the vicinity, he sent word through the village so that people could flee. If given enough advance warning, the entire village, taking provisions and using oxen to carry small children, headed for another village. If not, families grabbed some warm clothing and food, and made haste for a cave in the nearby hills. Soldiers on a mission to restock a troop's provisions could surprise. Several times, a terrified Tsan came face to face in the village with a *lo bak hao*—the Chinese of the south disparagingly nicknamed the Japanese *turnip heads*, after the long white root vegetable that was a staple of the enemy's diet. Tsan once watched some Japanese soldiers help themselves to the village's fattest pig, then roast it in plain sight of the family that owned it. Soldiers often tramped into houses at will, opening a family's coops and taking the chickens. Once, before marauding soldiers left the Hum house, several relieved themselves on the floor, creating a trail of filth.

Because of the war, the village school operated sporadically, closing temporarily or moving to another building, often even another village. After a year or so, Old Hum ended Tsan's formal schooling, deciding he had enough literacy and numeracy to start learning the business. He began to instruct Tsan on how to read the ledger of his accounts, including rent collections, payment of taxes and excises, and revenues from selling grain. "When you grow up," he told him, "you will do it all."

The grain dealer assigned Tsan the responsibility, which eventually became his alone, of accompanying his wife on twice-yearly collections from their tenant farmers, when the Hums took delivery of shares of their harvests as rent. The merchant's wife and Tsan set out in the pre-dawn, and went from village to village, across the Hums' landholdings near and far. With each tenant farmer, the two settled accounts, then employed local porters to carry the payment of grain to a hired boat moored on the river. Back at the family compound, by then nightfall, they employed more labourers to ferry the collected grain to the granary on the second floor of the house, where it awaited Old Hum's decision on the best time to sell and deliver to market.

Old Hum pledged to Tsan that in return for his labours, his position in the family would be secure: he would inherit two parcels of the family's land, fifty *mau* on the near side of the village, and fifty *mau* on the far side. He solemnly pointed out that, one day, his portrait would take its place of honour on the

Hum family's ancestral wall, where portraits of the couple's three deceased sons already hung. Tsan evaluated his life: They don't treat me badly. I'm not hungry, I have clothes to keep me warm. Yet he wished himself a different fate: I don't have a mother's love.

What little time Tsan had to himself came at sunset. He'd head for the village temple, knowing that at that hour he'd find old men taking in the view. They liked to talk to a child. Sometimes one would share a boiled wild sweet potato. Despite those stolen moments and their company, Tsan felt over-whelmed with loneliness. He tried to keep it at bay by holding fast to fading memories of his mother, his brother and sister, and his grandmother. Before bed, he prayed that they might wander through his dreams.

Within the Hum household, no one said a word about the family he'd left behind. No letters arrived for him, or if they did, the Hums didn't pass them on.

On one of his journeys to collect dues from tenant farmers, a lady who knew him by sight stopped him.

"I have a bit of news for you."

She said she had a son who went to school in the district market town. In such towns, which could serve as many as thirty satellite villages, stray bits of information about lost family members eventually found a nesting spot, in the way that swirling leaves settle into a pile.

The news was not good. Tsan's grandmother had succumbed some time ago to starvation. His mother, weakened by hunger, could hardly walk. Tsan asked after the welfare of his brother and sister. The woman knew nothing of their existence.

WHEN LIBERATION CAME in 1949, Tsan felt certain that trouble—big trouble—was coming. In the Hums' village and in villages where he collected grain payments, when the Kuomintang and the Communists had been fighting for control of the country, he had heard people chanting: "Kill Communists! Long live Chiang Kai-shek!"

When a new Communist order came to the Hums' village, local Communist Party cadres confiscated Old Hum's entire landholdings.

Expecting worse to come, Tsan decided not to wait around. Confident that the Hums, given the sudden chaos in their own lives, wouldn't care if he were to disappear, he made for Canton. In the crowded city, he could more easily disappear into anonymity. He found work in a barber shop, sweeping the floor and cooking for the boss, who let him sleep on a cot in the back. Within a year, the teenager was himself cutting hair. In his spare time, he strolled the streets taking note of storefronts with signs advertising courses in a trade. Once he'd saved enough money, he planned to come back and sign up for one of them.

Then one day, he had a surprise visitor at the barbershop.

His sister, by now married, had tracked him down. Overjoyed, Tsan asked after the rest of the family. She answered the mystery of why the woman on his grain collection route had known nothing of her or his brother: they were more often far away, as each walked great distances from home to find salt to buy, which they then carried home to resell for money to buy food. She reported that after the war ended with Japan, their brother and mother had fled to Hong Kong. When Liberation came and suddenly it was dangerous to be rich, their mother had asked the Hums to relinquish Tsan. Twice she asked, twice they refused. Then his sister learned that he had fled and she traced him, finally, to the barber shop in Canton. Six months later, Tsan had enough for a rail ticket to Hong Kong, where he was reunited with his family at last.

IN JANUARY 1956, Tsan bid goodbye to his mother, promising he'd send money regularly from Canada to support her and his brother and sister. She gave him a Canadian twenty-dollar bill, saved from years of *li shee*, that a nephew in Vancouver sent every Christmas. Tsan planned to spend it on stamps, to mail letters home from Canada.

Fourth Uncle met Tsan on arrival at the airport in Toronto and drove him not to London, as he'd expected, but rather to nearby Exeter. The town was best known for its canning factory that processed brand-name peas, corn, sauerkraut and tomatoes. Fourth Uncle owned a share in the Exeter Grill on the main street. He carried in Tsan's bag for him, dropped it on the floor and pointed up the stairs. "You live upstairs, you work downstairs," he said, then turned on his heel; he had to get back to his job as a cook at the hospital in London, thirty miles away. A moment later he reappeared: "One last thing, don't go out. You might get into a fist fight out there."

After a year of working seven days a week, and spending no money outside of haircuts and a movie or two, Tsan again lamented the utter loneliness of his life. He remained in penury and debt to Fourth Uncle, working off the cost of bringing him to Canada—seven hundred dollars for the air fare, plus eighteen hundred to buy the "slot" for a sponsored son. (The going rate was the age on the birth certificate times one hundred dollars.) Seeing no future for himself in Exeter and seeking an escape route, Tsan canvassed the other helpers in the kitchen. "Try to get into the United States; there's good money there," they said. This was wishful thinking at best. The United States had replaced exclusion with an annual quota that held Chinese immigration to a trickle.

Tsan asked his mother to obtain some addresses from a man in Hong Kong who had relations in their village and who was known to have sons and nephews in eastern Canada. Citing this acquaintance and a great-great-grandfather that they had in common, Tsan wrote to a restaurant owner, Stanley Wong of Ottawa, asking for work. A genial, refined and culti-vated gentleman, a skilled amateur actor and a chef, Stanley had realized his ambition of owning a restaurant that served Chinese cuisine when he and his part-Irish, part-Chinese wife, the former Marion Bristol Sinn, came with their young family from Montreal in 1941 to start the Canton Inn. The first restaurant to serve Chinese food in Ottawa, it remained a favourite haunt of diplomats and politicians. "Come on over to Ottawa," Stanley replied. He put Tsan up with the kitchen help in a dorm room above the Canton, and started him washing dishes, but quickly promoted him to kitchen helper, then cook's helper.

Stanley fell ill with a brain tumour that same year, in 1957. As his health rapidly deteriorated, he told his partners: "Tsan Wong is a good boy; make sure you keep him."

TSAN PUT ON A SUIT AND TIE, Brylcreemed his hair into a perfect wave, and headed down to the Chinese Mission. He called on the deaconess, Miss Ricker, and made a donation to the Sunday school—the fee for attending her remedial English classes on Wednesday evenings and Sunday afternoons. He also asked her to recommend a tutor for introductory French; he'd set his sights on earning a promotion to the Canton's dining room, and he wanted to extend a courtesy to politicians who were French-speaking of greeting them with "Bonjour, comment ça va."

What had propelled Tsan to the Mission was his mother's rebuff of his suggestion that he go to Hong Kong to look for a bride. In his letter, he named others in Ottawa who'd done the same. Like him, they knew they were out of the running when it came to Canadian-born Chinese girls. Tom-yee (Tom) Hum, for example, six years after emigrating from Hong Kong to Ottawa, went for a visit and returned with his new wife. Tsan had expected to hear that his mother was already lining up prospective wives. Instead, she wrote, "Don't come back to Hong Kong to marry, not yet. You're different than other boys. They are rich. You are not."

Tsan understood: Tom, his competition in the Hong Kong bride market, who had once waited on tables at the Ding Ho, could boast of owning a share of the Lucky Key Restaurant. That's when it struck Tsan. He'd been living in Canada for three years and had acquired almost no English. If he only spoke Chinese, not only was he never going to make it out of the kitchen; he would always be the lowest paid on staff.

SOME TIME LATER, at one of his English classes at the Chinese Mission, Tsan met a teenaged girl, newly arrived in Ottawa. He attended twice weekly; when she could make it, she came on Sunday afternoons. Before long, he was walking her home to her Auntie Eng's on Frank Street, where she minded the couple's four young children. Sometimes he walked her the long way around so that she could drop by her paper parents, whom she readily admitted she felt closer to. She confided that, like Tsan, she had entered Canada under a false identity; her real name was Lui-sang Hum. He began to court her, writing her letters. They'd take walks together around Dow's Lake near the Central Experimental Farm, or if they dared to splurge—both sent most of their pay cheques to family in Hong Kong—they treated themselves to a roast beef dinner at the Embassy Café.

Lui-sang's grandmother saw how happy the two were in each other's company. "He's a good boy," she told her grand-daughter, eyeing him as a prospective husband. She noted approvingly that, while Tsan Wong didn't yet own a house or a car, he had recently acquired a one-sixth share of the busy Canton Inn. Upon the death of its previous owner, Stanley Wong, the couple's only son, Donald, had taken over its management. But after two years, he'd told his mother, "It's not for me." On his deathbed, Stanley had said their son didn't have to take it on: "If he doesn't want to do it, please don't feel it has to be passed on." Stanley's widow sold the Canton to six of the staff, all of them either relations or, like Tsan, clansmen.

With some trepidation, Tsan wrote to his mother in Hong Kong to tell her of his impending marriage. "Don't worry," she wrote back. "Your brother and sister should soon be able to support themselves; you won't have to keep sending money home."

At the Chinese Mission, Miss Ricker happily took charge

of the arrangements. She was delighted, not to say chuffed, at this union of two people who had first met at her remedial English class. As with all her students, Miss Ricker had bestowed on them new Christian names, the better to help them make their way in a new country. Ever respectful of teachers, Tsan and Lui-sang readily agreed to the names she chose for them.

So it was that, come the wedding, Miss Ricker took care of the details of the service and personally made the white-bread rolled sandwiches, the cake and the squares that were served at the reception following. On the day, she put on her best dress, a hat and pearls, and when the photographer posed the wedding guests for a portrait with the bride and groom on the steps of the Mission, she joined in. In her mind, it was a pleasure to launch Gordon and Kathy into married life.

Agnes Lor and her five children: Alice (on her right) and Ruth (on her left) and (front, left to right) Joe, Gloria and Valerie. Others: Harry (Agnes's brother) and May, daughter of Leip Lor's first wife.

Courtesy Ruth Malloy

EIGHT

OUTCOMES

IN THE WINTER OF his last year of high school, Joe Lor wasn't sure what he'd do after he graduated, whether in the fall he'd go on to university and, if so, what he'd study. His three elder siblings had already gone out into the world. Alice had studied nursing at McGill, had married and was working in Toronto. Ruth had earned a bachelor's degree from the University of Toronto, was about to return to study social work, and had been a freelance writer and photographer, filing stories for the *Globe and Mail* from such far-flung places as Frobisher Bay in Canada's north and Brazil. Valerie was also in Toronto, in her second year at teachers' college. Only Joe and Gloria were still at home. At twelve, Gloria had a few years yet.

Like all the Lor children, Joe was born in Brockville. His first, and only, home was the apartment where his parents, Leip and Agnes, had begun their married life, above the New York Café. Their marriage and the family's restaurant were each going on thirty years.

Joe's older sisters had known that sooner rather than later they'd leave their hometown, if only because they weren't going to find husbands there. So he knew that life as he'd known it had to change. But comfortingly, during holidays and summers, when his sisters returned from university, their lives settled back into the rhythm of the family business. Just as the siblings did in their early childhood when they needed a parent to come upstairs to the apartment, one of them would take the broom, upend it, and bang on the floor to get the attention of a family member in the restaurant below. The five children still gravitated to the booth at the back, where they once did their homework, competing for space with their mother's paperwork and leaving their father to his office in the basement.

Perhaps when you're far down the sibling order, change comes harder. But that was thinking further ahead than Joe needed to. It was only February. He had a few more months to make any decision.

DESPITE LIVING IN A small town like Brockville, Joe had no sense that he was cut off from the world. In fact, the opposite was true. Come spring, once the ice broke up, the modern era of water transport, international commerce and tourism would sail into view. In a few weeks—as early as April—the recently completed St. Lawrence Seaway would open, linking the river with the five Great Lakes and the Atlantic Ocean. The official opening later this summer, on June 26, 1959, was going to be an international event, presided over by no less than Prime Minister John Diefenbaker, President Dwight Eisenhower and Queen Elizabeth.

The five years of construction to widen and deepen the channel between Montreal and Lake Ontario had been a mammoth spectacle in itself: the river had to be diverted to accommodate the building of locks and canals and, in advance of the controlled flooding, houses picked up and moved. But now that the seaway was finished, of all the river towns where one might watch the parade of ocean-going freighters, cruise ships and pleasure craft, Brockville arguably offered the best prospect; the river here was at its narrowest, less than a mile separating Ontario and New York State.

All of which boded well for business at the Lors' New York Café. Even before the seaway, one only had to see the volume of summertime traffic through town to recognize that Brockville attracted its share of tourists and big-city spenders. Its waterfront was a departure point for tours and cruises of the Thousand Islands, tree-covered granite hilltops of the southernmost reaches of the Canadian Shield that broke the water's surface. Thirty miles upriver, centred around Alexandria Bay, New York, these islands and the banks of the St. Lawrence were home to "Millionaires' Row," named for the summer mansions of industrialists and socialites from New York, Boston and Chicago who left city life behind and came for "the season."

Leip and Agnes Lor's New York Café was on King Street, a five-minute walk up from the tour boat pier at the end of Broad Street. Within a sixty-five-mile stretch of the King's Highway on the Canadian side, no fewer than five cafés, located in Brockville, Prescott, Morrisburg, Ganonoque and Iroquois, carried the same name, and were owned by Leip Lor or men related to him. He owned a share in three; he and his younger brother were sole proprietors of their own respective cafés.

Leip advertised his café as "The Largest Modern Restaurant on the St. Lawrence." He could stand by the claim: his 121–seat establishment was staffed, at its busiest, by six cooks, two dishwashers, seven waiters and two cashiers. The menu was beyond compare. Within its pages, one could find the standard fare of

"Americanized" Chinese food, from chicken balls (but made with delicate coatings that drew raves) to chow mein (including the perennial favourite, the chow mein bun). But as well, it offered cuisine that one would expect to find in the dining rooms of storied resorts and grand hotels, including Malpeque Oysters Rockefeller and seared Nova Scotia sea scallops, and smoked Winnipeg Goldeye. Leip put his signature on his restaurant with the menu's daily specials, deciding them the night before, according to what he'd bought and had shipped in or what was in season. If venison or bear steak, he had paid a hunter for them. If lamb chops, a local sheep farmer had raised the lamb and butchered it. If sturgeon, an angler had taken it from the St. Lawrence River; if whitefish, from Lake Ontario. Even the frog's legs were from frogs trapped in the nearby countryside.

Sophisticated diners would recognize Leip's restaurant as belonging to the tradition first made famous by Ruby Foo's in Boston. Tired of virulent anti-Chinese sentiment on North America's west coast, Ruby decamped from San Francisco and in 1923 opened Ruby Foo's Den in Boston's Chinatown. Her clientele were well-heeled Jewish families, many of whom managed or owned garment factories. Where timing is everything, Ruby hit the jackpot. First- and second-generation Jews, whose families had emigrated from European cities, saw dining out as a way to indulge their refined palates. Chinese cooking, which never combined dairy with meat, relied on clear broths, and allowed forbidden pork to disappear into say, an egg roll, sat comfortably with Jewish dietary customs. And, "eating Chinese" was at once a compelling bargain and a cosmopolitan experience. Ruby went on to open four more Ruby Foo's restaurants, including, most recently, one in Montreal in 1945.

A similar attraction drew crowds to Leip Lor's New York Café. Even the "mileage card"—the souvenir calling card handed out to patrons—suggested one had *arrived*. On the flip side of a photograph of the posh dining room, with its checkered floor, glass pendant lamps and ceiling fan, a detailed chart set out "DISTANCES FROM BROCKVILLE," listing mileage from fifty-one cities, towns and villages. Some were as far away as Quebec City and Chicago. Some were only fifteen minutes down the highway: Prescott on the Canadian side, or directly opposite, reachable by a year-round ferry, Ogdensburg on the American side.

THE LORS' RESTAURANT, open everyday of the year except Christmas Day, opened at half past eight in the mornings, and closed at half past eleven in the evenings Monday to Saturday and at ten on Sundays. The only respite in the long workday came mid-afternoon, when the restaurant closed in the interval between lunch and dinner. In summer, Leip would pile some of the family into his beat-up Dodge and they'd escape to their cottage four miles down the road for a swim or to fish off the dock. By late afternoon, one of them had to be back at the restaurant. The Lors had one standing rule: during opening hours one family member—the children counted, once they were old enough—had to be on the premises. The rule held even when Agnes's beloved brother Charlie died. One of the daughters was designated to stay behind while the rest of the family went overnight to North Bay for the funeral.

On this cold February day, during the afternoon break, Joe wandered into the living room and came upon his father stretched out on the sofa. Maybe he was tired; how could he not be.

"Joe, would you play the piano for me?"

Joe felt honoured by his father's request. His mother had been the one to insist that each of the children take piano lessons, which for five had been no small expense. The practising over the years had taken its toll on the piano; each end of the keyboard was missing two keys. Joe pulled back the stool, sat himself comfortably, and considered what to play from his repertoire of the Grade 9 syllabus of the Royal Conservatory of Music. He chose a Bach piece, as the composer's music seemed both calming and meditative. If played well, Bach's music would show off his dedication and hours of practice, virtues that his father would appreciate.

When Joe's performance ended, Leip expressed his gratitude. Joe rose, pushed the stool back in place, and told his father he was going out to get some air. His father responded by saying, "If anything happens, promise me you'll make sure you take care of your mother." Odd thing for Dad to say, Joe thought. He grabbed his winter coat, planning to walk over to Delaney's Bowling Alley to see if anybody he knew might be hanging out at the pool tables there.

LEIP LOR'S SUCCESS IN Brockville followed on that of his father, who'd brought him to Canada and later returned to China in the same year that Leip married Agnes. In 1909, father and son had been toiling, unhappily, in Havana, Cuba, when a compatriot from a neighbouring village in China, who had a laundry in Brockville, got word to him that the city had room for a second laundry. Settled by United Empire Loyalists who escaped the American Revolution by coming north, Brockville, the first city to be incorporated in Ontario—in

1832—boasted an array of factories on its waterfront, from tinsmiths to shipbuilding.

The elder Lor paid the Canadian head tax for himself and his twelve-year-old son, and opened Kwong Sing Laundry at the cheaper-rent end of King Street. His sign promised "First Class Service," and to win his customers' confidence, he attired his bachelor workers in immaculate white shirts and crisply pressed trousers. He allowed Leip two years of schooling, then put him to work in the laundry. When the elder Lor sold out twenty years later, he passed his investments of a piggery and some land near Brockville to his son.

By then, Leip had shifted his own obligations from China to Canada. He'd followed the familiar pattern of marriage in China, leaving behind a pregnant wife on his return to Canada. Shortly after the birth of a daughter, his wife died, leaving relatives to raise their child. A decade later, Leip decided he wanted to remarry in Canada. He asked a friend in the missionary society to help find him a Chinese wife, and a contact at the Presbyterian Church in North Bay turned up Agnes Young, a tall, striking girl with the posture of a dancer. She was twenty, twelve years Leip's junior. After corresponding for a few months, the two married. Leip was impressed by her evident cleverness; Agnes was persuaded that "since he's a Christian, he must be okay."

From the start, Leip and Agnes divided the responsibilities in their new restaurant. Leip, the face of the business, ran the kitchen. He dealt with the cooks and did all the buying, travelling every few weeks to Montreal, sometimes including a side trip to Ottawa. In Montreal, he picked up general delivery mail destined for various relations and bachelors. On his way back, he'd stop to deliver it at their cafés and laundries.

Agnes focused on the customers. She scheduled the wait-ers and cashiers, did the payroll, and at close of day balanced the day's cash receipts and transactions, staying up half the night if necessary to get it right. And, once Leip decided the next day's specials, she typed the daily menu insert, which she then left for one of the children to copy on the Gestetner machine in the morning, the only time they ventured into their father's basement office.

The personalities of this husband and wife team appeared to be complementary: Leip was outgoing, with a loud and resonant voice—he was capable of raising it to astounding volumes—to match his sociable, cigar-smoking ways. Agnes was charming, soft-spoken, both self-assured and shy. Yet when it came to the business, they were highly competitive. Leip had great confidence in his business acumen, as she did in her own. Like his family's success, hers had been proven over two generations. Her family's road from China to Canada had travelled through Philadelphia and Boston, where her father had been a merchant, and then to Montreal and finally North Bay, where he'd opened a laundry and a café. When Agnes was five, her mother, newly widowed, took her young family back to China, thinking she could stretch the family's savings further there, only to decide two years later that a better future for her children lay back in the restaurant and laundry in North Bay. With her encouragement, Agnes would graduate from a business college in North Bay, and work as a secretary at a local insurance company.

Leip, mostly self-educated, had the equivalent of an eighth-grade education, well short of what Agnes had achieved. But when it came to business, he relied on intuition and gut feeling. Agnes prided herself on constantly thinking of ways to "improve" the family's business. She relished checking out the competition. Whenever she took shopping trips to Montreal, she dined at Chinese-owned restaurants. If Ruth was along, she would pen "reviews" for her mother.

As stubborn as Leip was about giving ground on any matter, Agnes never held back on her opinions. The two clashed often, their arguments sometimes erupting into loud and prolonged rows. The Lor children accepted this tension between their parents, as if their reliably opposed opinions created the vitality and energy that kept the café thriving.

"EVERYONE KNOWS OUR FAMILY," Agnes reminded her children. "Your father is respected in this town." As a newlywed, Agnes had been impressed that people tipped their hat to her husband. And not just ordinary folk, but police, lawyers and judges. After hours, the police would invite Leip to ride along with them on their patrols. He's famous, trusted and well liked, Agnes noted. And he was a leader. Leip was elected head of the local business association and was often quoted in the *Brockville Recorder and Times.* Agnes, always stylishly attired in an outfit that showed off her trim waist, with her hair swept up in a chignon, forbade her daughters from wearing shorts or baring their arms in public. Each time an adult they didn't recognize passed them on the sidewalk with a "Hello, Miss Lor," the daughters had to concede the wisdom of their mother's lessons in modesty. In case Agnes missed something in teaching her children social graces she instructed them: "When you go to white people's homes, watch what they do." In North Bay, she had benefited from the tutoring of a proper English family.

The most telling way in which the Lors resembled a typical upstanding middle-class family was their participation in the church. As superintendent of Sunday school at First Presbyterian Church, Leip expected his children to earn perfect attendance certificates, and later, to teach classes themselves. All sang in the church choir. Joe took part in the minister's bible class for teenage boys. Leip demanded piety on Sundays, forbidding his children to read comic books on that day. When he could, he attended Sunday service. Agnes, though devout, preferred to be the one who stayed behind at the restaurant. There were music lessons—piano, violin and organ—the girls joined Girl Guides and Christian Girls in Training, and Joe, cubs, then scouts. Gloria took figure-skating lessons (her talent eventually landing her a career with the Ice Capades). There was a family dog—named Judy. Games of cards—Agnes liked canasta—and Monopoly were played on the living room floor. There were annual forays to get a Christmas tree. In summer, Agnes cut flowers and harvested vegetables from her large garden.

Leip bought a waterfront lot because Agnes said she longed to have a cottage for the children to grow up with. He hired Bob Brown, a farmer whom he used as a handyman at the restaurant, to help him organize the building of a cabin and a dock. Every spring, Leip and the children put in the dock, hung the life buoy and took the boats out of storage. He put in the raft that he'd built himself, anchoring it offshore. Sometimes he took one of the children and set out with his shotgun to go duck hunting. Once he'd gone with another hunter in town after bear, and returned to regale the children with a story of how he got chased up a tree.

———

THE LOR CHILDREN CAME to take exception to one singular difference between them and their school friends: their friends had idle hours to meet up and do as they liked. The Lors couldn't remember a time when they didn't have to work at the restaurant. From the age of four or five, they were required to help with the laundry, done in the basement. The younger ones shook out the wet linen napkins, the older siblings hung them alongside the tablecloths on the clothesline. As the children became capable of heavier work, like washing, and then dangerous work, like ironing, their chores increased. Upstairs at the restaurant, they folded napkins, laid tablecloths and set the tables. When they could add and subtract, they worked the cash register. If they were too short to reach, they stood on a chair. When they were older still, they waited on tables, not only on weekends, but after school and, on very busy days, over the lunch hour.

There was one Chinese custom that the Lor children hoped their white friends would never learn about: the annual gathering of Chinese at the Brockville Cemetery. Tomb-sweeping day—the ritual of cleaning the tombstones, clearing the ground of weeds and, finally, sharing food that is first offered to the dead—is traditionally carried out around the full moon in the third lunar month. In Canada, spring's later arrival pushed the rites into May. On the day, about twenty-five Chinese from around Brockville came loaded down with cooked dishes (one year, Leip arranged a barbecued pig from Montreal). The crowd, mostly men, many in jacket and tie, and the women, decked out in hats, headed for "Potter's Field," the section of the Protestant cemeteries set aside for those who died destitute or without kin, stillborn babies and convicts.

Amid the overgrowth of tall grass, Leip, standing in for all sons of ancestors, laid out an offering of a steamed whole chicken, roast pork, rice, fruit, tea, chopsticks, bowls and cups. He bowed three times, then trickled a bottle of Johnny Walker Red Label around the few lonely tombstones with Chinese inscriptions. Before the crowd sat down for a picnic, one ritual remained: Leip took out the pistol he'd brought and fired a single shot into the air, alerting the dead that the living were here to pay their respects and to scare off evil spirits. Only once before, one December 31, had the pistol come out. At midnight (he notified the police beforehand), his pistol shot was the signal for the festivities and feasting to begin.

Apart from this annual visit to the cemetery, the Lor children's sense of their Chinese origins faded early on. Agnes and Leip would have liked them to read and write Chinese, but neither had the time to teach them. Once, Leip hired a tutor for the older girls, but gave up when they refused to cooperate. That their parents harboured foreign traditions emerged sporadically, such as the time Agnes boiled chicken feathers to make a solution to soothe an itch for Valerie. Or when Leip showed them the bear claw he'd added to one of his health tonics, herbs infused with alcohol, lined up in large jars that previously held supplies for the restaurant. Or, more frequently, when their father, in an exuberant mood, would wake the entire family to join him in *siu-yeh,* the Chinese tradition of a shared late-night meal. But the children saw those occasions more in terms of their father's deciding to cook something special, like oysters, breaking his rule of certain foods on the menu being exclusively for customers.

Still, one connection remained to the family's shared

Chinese roots: the bachelors who worked as kitchen help. The third floor was given over to a dorm for them, but they used a separate back staircase to access it. The children knew none by name, as they addressed them only by the appropriate Chinese titles of respect, which defer to age. Their limited acquaintance with the bachelors came by way of the red envelopes of *li shee* at Chinese New Year's which the children deposited into their savings accounts, or else by snippets of the bachelors' conversations that drifted from their stairwell as they passed by the door off the Lors' eating area—mostly regret about gambling losses at mahjong—which the children hardly understood with their scant knowledge of Chinese.

All in all, the Lor children considered themselves to be as Canadian as any other family in Brockville. It came as a surprise, then, to the older girls, once they came into their teenage years, to realize that the only boys who befriended them were those whom they happened to be seated beside in class. Never did a boy ask them to a school social or dance, and sadly, they understood that it was never going to happen. Apparently there was no avoiding how boys their age, or the boys' parents, saw them: the Lor girls were Chinese. Suddenly they were on par with another family in Brockville that they had considered they had nothing in common with, the city's only other Chinese family, the Wongs, a couple with adult children who ran Diana Sweets Café. The realization unearthed a memory of boys yelling "Chinky, Chinky Chinaman!" at them when they were little. "They're ignorant," Agnes had advised. "If they stare at you, stare back."

I hate being Chinese, the girls told each other.

———

AT DELANEY'S BOWLING ALLEY, one of the friends that Joe met there suggested they go for beers "across the bay," code for crossing the river to the village of Morristown on the American side. In New York State the boys were legal. The minimum drinking age there was eighteen; in Ontario, it was twenty-one. All four boys were up for it, until someone suggested that they walk across the ice.

One of them balked.

Had it been January, a month earlier, he'd have been game. A prolonged cold snap could freeze the river at Brockville from one bank to the other. Back in the 1940s, people routinely walked across to avoid paying for the horse-drawn sleigh ferry that operated between Morristown and Brockville.

But this winter had not been a severe one. By late February, with fluctuating temperatures creating pockets of open water, to walk clear across was tempting fate. To go by road over to the other side involved taking the Prescott–Ogdensburg ferry, which ran year-round, then doubling back to Morristown.

"Two cases of beer if we make it."

"There and back?"

The bet was on. Joe and two of his friends set out.

NONE OF THE FAMILY COULD identify when Leip came to find comfort in a nip of alcohol; a bottle of whisky or rye had always stood alongside his health tonics. Nor did they know which came first, his bouts of depression or his propensity for drink. Whatever the trigger, Leip could go from happiness to anger, even fury, as if a light switch had been flipped.

The rest of the family found it downright bizarre the time he took on the entire family at once. Agnes and the children were having dinner in the kitchen when they heard Leip pound up the stairs. He burst in and tore into them, yelling about all he had to do for them, even wash their dirty laundry. He lambasted them as if they were all lazy and slothful. His booming voice ricocheted off the walls: "I have to do everything for you, as well as do everything else around here!"

As it was, Leip was always at the children about their chores and how when he was their age he had to work sixteen-hour days, seven days a week. While the girls heard it as nagging, Joe was more sympathetic. He saw it as his father trying to instill the value of hard work and reminding them that money was hard-earned.

But most disconcerting about this particular outburst aimed at them was Leip's plaintive plea before he headed back downstairs: "Help me."

The family started to worry. Agnes and the older girls finally broached the possibility of a drinking problem with Leip. In the early 1940s, the notion of addiction made news when a fellowship called Alcoholics Anonymous came north over the border into Ontario. The older girls heard that a branch had started up in Toronto and they tried to persuade their father to go, but he refused.

In spite of her husband's unpredictable moods, Agnes was steadfast in her efforts to have father and son bond. "Take Joe with you," she'd say to Leip. Joe, whose temperament took after his mother's, saw just how keen she was when she took him out of school so that he could accompany his father on a two-day trip to Montreal, when he was scouting chefs to hire.

When he spent time with his father, typically fishing or hunting, Joe came to take for granted the bottle his father kept handy in his pocket.

On one such afternoon, the two were out on the water and readying their fishing rods. Joe watched his father and as he would have predicted, Leip choose the heaviest sinker.

Joe decided to ask why, to see what his father would say.

"Because no fish is going to want to fight me after being on that sinker!"

"Aren't we here to enjoy fishing?"

"We're here to CATCH FISH!"

This is so silly, thought Joe. My father sees life as one fight after another. "Well, I want to give that fish a fighting chance!"

When the older girls again raised with their mother their father's drinking, Agnes tried to brush off their worries: "Your father only drinks beer now." Leip's flashes of temper seemed to have subsided. He more often took to lying down and napping, though maybe sleep was due to having a drink; or perhaps it was the other way around, that he'd taken a drink to bring it on.

IN THE SPRING OF 1954, Ruth had a newly minted degree in psychology from the University of Toronto. That same year, the Canadian economy took an unexpected dip. For businesses and residents along the St. Lawrence, a sudden pessimism nationwide about the country's economic outlook came just as they had to contend with disruption from the construction of the seaway. At school's end, instead of returning to Brockville, Ruth travelled to Washington, D.C., to participate in a workshop on non-violent ways to end racial discrimination.

Her mother would not be impressed.

Ruth's workshop, which she'd applied for and won a scholarship to attend, was led by Wallace Nelson, a prominent civil rights activist. Wallace had been one of a team that undertook a "Journey for Reconciliation" in 1947, riding interstate buses in the Deep South to test the Supreme Court's ruling against segregated buses for travel between states. Using that as a model, Ruth's colleagues visited restaurants, theatres and swimming pools to test access for blacks. Repeatedly, they were arrested and jailed, making national news.

To Ruth's disappointment, her mother wrote chastising her for not coming home to help at the restaurant. It was not the first time that she'd gone against her mother's wishes. When Ruth had completed high school, at Agnes's urging she'd enrolled in a secretarial course at a business college in Brockville. But, as she confided to her sister Alice, the courses bored her. On a whim, Alice put her sister's name on a raffle ticket she'd bought to raise money to rebuild the rink at the Brockville Memorial Civic Centre. Ruth won the grand prize, a new Chevrolet, and promptly sold it, using the proceeds to go to university.

In reply to her mother, Ruth made an impassioned argument for the need to advance civil rights in the United States, which she declared had relevance for Canadian society. Three single-spaced typed pages later, she wrote: "With my intelligence, I can find few better fields to put my education to use." Having warmed up her typewriter, Ruth let her indignation fly.

I do not understand your phrase: "so far Daddy has helped to give you and Alice a career education, and so far he has not had any returns when he needed it most—it does prove discouraging." What is it that you require of me? If it is money, why do you recommend that I work a year, earn enough money to carry me through further studies? How can I send money home if I am to save for studies. If it is that you want me home to work in the restaurant, this recommendation doesn't follow either. Besides, I doubt if Daddy would give me a reasonable amount of responsibility in the restaurant as I would refuse to work otherwise. I cannot be a puppet, which is what I am every time I come home to work in the restaurant. This may sound rather blunt, but I say this with all humility and love, believe me. I cannot be a puppet and at the same time a creative human being.

IN THE OPINION OF AN OUTSIDER, Leip Lor's café in Brockville was an anomaly. "Odd that their business is always booming," Mabel Johnston said to her daughter Doris. "Of course, I don't have any of the Lors' expensive dishes on the menu."

After the sudden drop in 1954, the economy had picked right back up. Yet, Mabel noticed, her business was falling off. Why, she couldn't understand. People didn't seem to be going out to eat as they once were; maybe they were enthralled with television, or maybe they were spending their money in other ways, on automatic clothes washing machines and tumble dryers.

She tried to take a lesson from her late husband's nose for opportunity. She remembered how Harry had thought it unusual that American children attending Camp Shomira, the Jewish summer camp on Otty Lake, who came in at day's end for a candy bar and a soft drink, always left a tip, something Canadian children would never do. He decided to go after the business of their parents when they came on weekends to visit their children. "Jewish people won't eat a pork chop, but I know they like veal," he told Mabel.

Mabel had the idea that she could add to the tourists' experience by giving away chopsticks. The thought was that they'd keep them, and remember Harry's Café and come back or advertise for her, but she stopped her experiment when she didn't see any difference in the traffic to the restaurant.

How could Leip Lor afford to source the food he offered, she wondered. Local lamb was trouble enough, never mind trying to arrange for fresh lobsters and oysters. Mabel put it down to the Lors' clientele: "They get all the high-class tourist business up and down the river. They know what the tourists want—expensive, good food."

KEEPING TO WHAT TRACES remained of a walking path across the ice, Joe and his two friends made it to the other side. They scrambled up the riverbank and began to walk along the isolated stretch of River Road toward Morristown. They came upon a driver whose car was stuck in a snowbank. The boys offered to help the man and after some effort, they managed to free his car.

Having heard that the boys had walked across the ice from Brockville, the man said that if they were returning the same way, they ought to be thinking about going back as it was getting late. Perhaps the man was concerned that the waning light of day would make a crossing by foot even more treacherous.

In the sobering presence of an adult, the boys, burying their teenage bravado, agreed among themselves that they ought to take the Ogdensburg ferry back.

"Can we hitch a ride into town?"

"How about I take you right to the ferry?"

The man drove through Morristown. Short of Ogdensburg, he stopped at the border-crossing office of U.S. Customs and Immigration. "I'm turning you boys in."

Joe wondered if the man had double-crossed him and his friends because he had something against the Chinese.

Fortunately, all the boys, including Joe, happened to have border-crossing cards on them. It was common to live on one side and work or have businesses on the other, so locals on both sides of the river were accustomed to crossing freely without need to show a card.

Only Joe was taken into an interrogation room. He produced his card. Silently he thanked his father; when the United States and Canada ordered the internment of those of Japanese descent, Leip had taken out cards for all his children: "Just in case someone mistakes you for Japanese."

Two hours later, Joe finally emerged to rejoin his friends. "You're being deported," an official told the three, putting them in a car and making sure they boarded the ferry in Ogdensburg.

By the time Joe reached King Street in Brockville, it was twilight. He was late. He should have been back well before five, to help out at the restaurant. He noticed that the restaurant's neon sign, with its more than two hundred bulbs surrounding the letters spelling out the name of the café, wasn't lit. Something has to be wrong, he thought. Years ago, Joe's father invested in a generator to make sure the sign could always be lit. Of course, his parents argued about that. Agnes said the kitchen ought to have first claim on the generator. "The sign is more important!" Leip thundered.

Joe hurried his step. He started up the stairs, but before he reached the top, his mother appeared.

At the sight of her slumped shoulders, Joe knew that whatever it was, it was terrible news.

"He used a gun."

Agnes said it happened at four o'clock. One of the bachelors working in the kitchen had heard the muffled shot of the pistol, run downstairs to the basement and found Leip's body in his office.

Agnes and Gloria had been upstairs in the apartment but they hadn't seen Leip go downstairs; nor had the kitchen help seen him go down the basement. He could have gone unnoticed, if he'd used the back staircase and the outside entrance to the basement.

Nobody but Leip ever went into the backroom of the basement where he stored his guns in a locked cabinet. The rest of the family regarded it as a storeroom of "expensive Chinese stuff." It held porcelain and rosewood carvings, mostly deities and buddhas, the provenance of which was forgotten, likely left behind by Leip's father.

TWO DAYS BEFORE THE FUNERAL, Agnes, sorting through her husband's papers in his office, made a startling discovery. The New York Café owed its creditors a hundred and twenty thousand dollars.

Struggling to understand why her husband had been driven to take his own life, Agnes told Joe of an unsettling incident that she'd recently witnessed. She'd gone into the kitchen of the restaurant and happened upon Leip having a run-in with one of his chefs.

"You're not my boss," the chef sneered.

Having to put up with such lip from chefs was part and parcel of owning a restaurant. Chefs were a temperamental lot, given to fits of pique. Jack Sim, whose success at running his restaurants in Hull and Ottawa got him elected head of the Canadian Restaurant Association, always said that staff was the biggest challenge in the business, and that of all the staff, the kitchen was the most troublesome: "Say something wrong to the chefs, and they take off their apron and they're gone."

"I could buy you out tomorrow," the chef taunted.

Normally, Leip would have given back as good as he got, his voice alone commanding authority. He said, quietly, "Go to hell."

How had the tables turned? Agnes and Joe spoke of how Leip had rescued many a bachelor trapped here by exclusion and the war, or down on their luck. From the days when he had a laundry, he'd given them a meal and a bed and often, work. Some had lived on the third floor for decades.

Agnes raised with Joe the only option she saw for the restaurant: to declare bankruptcy.

Joe thought of what "taking care" of his mother meant. I better hang around here, he told himself. Bankruptcy would leave his mother with nothing. "I'll put off school," he said. "I want to do it." They both knew what he meant; he'd help her prove that she could run the restaurant.

Agnes was suddenly optimistic. "None of your dad's creditors are going to run us out of town."

A thousand people filled First Presbyterian Church to over-flowing for Leip Lor's funeral. It reached Agnes's ears that the wife of her husband's brother with the café in Gananoque was telling relatives that Agnes drove her husband to his death, because she hadn't behaved like a good Chinese wife.

Days later, Joe stood amid the dust of renovations at the restaurant. He and Agnes, accepting that people could be superstitious about where a suicide has taken place, had agreed that he ought to make the place look different. Joe began by ripping out the booths, but he left the partition hinges on the walls, as if leaving an artifact of his father's time.

It would take Agnes three years to turn the restaurant around and clear the debt.

TO BRING A STEADY INCOME into the family while still saving for university, Joe applied for a job that fall at one of Brockville's largest manufacturing plants. Phillips Cables pro-duced copper rods and insulated wires and cables. Its two-hundred-foot smokestack was a landmark in Eastern Ontario. A manager hired Joe on condition that the plant's doctor certify that he was in good health.

The doctor warned the new employee that work on the factory floor was not easy: "You know, Joe, it's not going to be like working in the family restaurant. White people live differently."

Joe was hired on for thirty-nine dollars a week. He worked a shift from Monday to Friday, which left his evenings and weekends free to help out at the restaurant. He decided that the doctor at Phillips Cables was right: working in the factory was different; it was a lot easier than working at the restaurant.

Janet and Golden Lang and their infant daughter,
Arlene, and Golden's parents.

Courtesy Golden Lang

NINE

RESOLVE

ON THE PLANE'S DESCENT, a stewardess announced that Anchorage would be a refuelling stop only. The flight, which had originated in Hong Kong, was en route to Vancouver. Janet peered out the window at the ground below. She could see nothing to suggest a human landscape—not a building, not a person, nothing but whiteness. She could not even make out where the sky met the ground.

Please don't tell me I've died, she prayed. Don't tell me this is heaven.

All around her sat strangers. She included her new husband, seated beside her, in that category.

"That's snow down there," he told her.

So God wasn't at hand after all. Still, she hoped she wasn't going to end up in a place like this.

At least she would have a few things to remind her of the life she'd left behind. In Hong Kong, when she'd been packing to go abroad, her new husband had invited her to make use of room in his luggage. Earlier that summer, he'd flown from Ottawa for their wedding and had brought two oversized suit-cases, one of which he'd deliberately left half empty. Janet took a last look to see what else she'd like to take. She regretted most that marriage had cut short her schooling, all the more so because her parents had not enrolled her until she was ten. She'd only had six years of school. Her elder sister had shrugged off her complaint: "We all started late." Only the two youngest of the five siblings—the boys—had been educated from an early age. Into the space in her husband's suitcase, Janet crammed what she could fit of her school texts, novels and magazines.

Even now, halfway to her destination on the other side of Canada, she felt as if she was not Janet Tang, the sixteen-year-old girl who'd only known city life, but another girl who'd been abruptly plucked from school and a month later married off to Golden Lang, twenty-one, originally from a village on the mainland, in China.

Perhaps the reality of her situation was all the harder to grasp because her mother, when speaking to Golden, continually used the third person to refer to her, even when she was standing right there.

In the two months between the wedding and the young couple's departure for Canada, on September 3, 1955, Mrs. Tang had taken charge of preparations for her daughter to set up house abroad. But as it turned out, Golden didn't think his parents, who owned and ran a café near Ottawa, and with whom he and Janet would be living, lacked for anything.

"What about dishes? Every bride should at least have dishes in her dowry."

"We have everything at home."

"What about chopsticks?"

"No, no, we have lots of stuff like that."

"Will she need some good dresses?" asked Janet's mother,

by which she meant *cheong sams*. No, said Golden, giving Janet her first hint that her life was about to take a direction very different from how she'd lived in Hong Kong, the city of her birth.

Nonetheless, Mrs. Tang filled Janet's trunk with a new wardrobe. She took her to the tailor, who made up some padded silk jackets intended to keep her warm against the cold in Canada, and as well, a dozen stylish "American" outfits in different colours. Mrs. Tang bought crinolines to be worn with full, gathered skirts, and a dozen pairs of high-heeled shoes.

Janet contemplated the stark landscape outside the plane window and was suddenly glad of what, at the last minute, she'd thought to add to her luggage. She had run downstairs from their high-rise apartment to the busy street, where any number of shops sold porcelain figurines of *Fook, Luk, Sau*, the three immortals who represented everything one could want from life. Most every home displayed them; if properly placed, the three rested at a height no lower than shoulder level and in a position where they could cast their eyes upon those entering a room.

Janet bought a small, cheap set. Each figurine, only three inches high, was a traditionally depicted replica. *Fook*, a scholar in a turquoise robe, held a baby, symbolizing the harmony that comes with continuing the lineage of family; *Luk*, clad in the rich red robes of a mandarin, carried the sceptre of office, conveying authority and prosperity; and *Sau*, an old man, his walking stick enfolded in his yellow robe, carried a peach, the fruit of immortality.

Not knowing what to expect of the landscape where the Langs lived, Janet considered the secondary purpose of her three celestial deities: as long as she acknowledged that any goodness that came her way was their doing, they would also dispel any hovering bad luck.

THE DEAL BETWEEN Mrs. Tang in Hong Kong and Mrs. Lang in Canada to marry their children to each other had been struck five years earlier. The Tangs had fled their village ahead of the Japanese, and Mr. Tang had re-established himself in Hong Kong with a taxi business. In 1950, Mrs. Lang had in turn made her way from a neighbouring village to Hong Kong, where she awaited approval from Canadian Immigration to join her husband, a cook at a café in Quebec. The Langs' third child, Golden, then aged sixteen and the only one of their offspring young enough to qualify as a dependent child, had gone on several months ahead.

Upon meeting in Hong Kong, the two women agreed that five years later, when Golden turned twenty-one, he would return from Canada to marry Mrs. Tang's eldest daughter. When the time came to honour the agreement, Golden flew to Hong Kong. However, the Tangs' daughter, by then nineteen, refused to give up her boyfriend. The mothers then agreed that the Tangs could substitute their second daughter. When that daughter proved even more obstinate than the first, Mrs. Tang promised that by the wedding date set in eight weeks' time, she would deliver her youngest daughter to the altar.

Mrs. Tang informed Janet that the ceremony would be at the marriage bureau in Hong Kong's government offices; Golden was not a Christian. If Janet's family, members of the Congregation of Christ Church (restored after the Japanese had used it as a horse stable), could not give her a church ceremony, they did orchestrate a formal wedding portrait. The bride, eschewing the traditional *cheong sam* for a white wedding gown, had one attendant—her cousin—and the groom had five—her father's chauffeur, her two brothers and her two younger cousins.

It had not occurred to Janet, a fine-boned, pretty girl, when first told her fate, to protest as her older sisters later told her they had done. Nor did anyone explain what to expect of her domestic life in Canada with her new in-laws. At home in Hong Kong, she'd never so much as boiled water or washed a pair of socks; her family had servants to cook, clean and do the laundry. Janet put no such questions to Golden, whose baby fat made him look more boy than man, and he himself volunteered nothing.

SINCE HIS FAMILY didn't own a car, Golden had arranged for Clifford Cox, a retired farmer who sold life insurance, to meet him and his new wife at Ottawa Airport. The ride twenty-five miles west on Highway 17, skirting the city of Ottawa and passing by farmers' fields dotted with solitary trees, took them to the village of Carp. There, the road, part of the new Trans-Canada Highway, turned into Main Street. A cluster of modest wood-sided houses delineated the village from the surrounding farms. As evident from the outhouses in the backyards, few had indoor plumbing. At the far end of the village, beyond an archway proclaiming the "Carp Agricultural Society," stood a landmark of the county: a massive red octagonal barn, where, come time for the annual Carp Fair, farmers and their wives presented their best, from show horses and cattle to giant pumpkins and home-baked pies.

At a red and green sign that read "BA"—for British American Oil Company—Mr. Cox pulled into an expansive gravel lot. A long, flat-roofed single-storey building, an addition to a barn, sat back from two gas pumps. On the wall closest to the barn hung a noisy confusion of signs. The largest, anchored by DRINK COCA-COLA at either end, read GOLDEN CAFE. A faded board indicated RESTAURANT, and another, SNACK BAR. The door to the café extolled the fresh taste of PURE SPRING ginger ale. Mr. Cox stopped the car in front of a tiny porch on the far side. If only by the absence of signage, that half of the addition was identifiable as the café's adjoining living quarters.

A wave of disappointment washed over Janet. In her naïveté, she had assumed that Golden's parents lived in a city like Hong Kong with high-rises, trams and taxis, and a street life that carried on day and night. Where were all the people? This place is empty farmland, she thought: I've gone back fifty years.

For the next three years, hardly a day would go by that Janet didn't dissolve in tears. Convinced that her mother had married her off to "get rid" of her, especially since her family rarely bothered to write, she confided nothing in her obligatory letters home. Of this she was certain: nobody living with her knew of her sadness.

"We have everything at home," Golden had said in Hong Kong. But Janet saw that "everything" turned out to be chopsticks and little else. But rarely did they come out. The family habitually ate whatever her father-in-law, who did most of the cooking, had prepared on the café side—their only kitchen. That meant hamburger steak with mashed potatoes, gravy and carrots. In summer, he sometimes cooked a stir-fry for the family from the *bok choy, lo bok,* snow peas and swiss chard that he harvested from his garden out back, but he saved most of the space for lettuce, tomatoes, beans and carrots for the café. The rare luxury of rice was dulled by having to eat from the heavy white dishes used at the café.

What bonded the family was constant work, seven days a week. Besides staffing the café and gas pumps, someone had to meet the Colonial Coach buses when they came through, twice a day in each direction, on their Ottawa–Toronto route; the company paid the Langs to accept parcels, to be given to the driver. At the same time, the buses discharged passengers as anxious to use the café washroom as to buy candies and drinks and snacks during the short rest stop. Then there was the housekeeping and laundry, the garden to tend; and in the cold weather, the stove on the café side to be stoked with wood by day and coal by night, and the front door and the gas pump area cleared of snow. Plus, the Langs had duties as landlords. They rented out the barn—for now, to a neighbour who used it to park his Canada Bread delivery truck—and two small apartments behind the family's rooms, where the land fell away toward the river then rose to the railway track. The apartments attracted transients, who often disappeared in the night, leaving rent unpaid; or sometimes had to be evicted for fear their rowdiness and drunken behaviour would offend the neighbours, with their strict Presbyterian attitudes. Carp was a "dry" town.

Except for the reading material she'd brought, and read many times over, Janet found little diversion in the village. Its only other commercial enterprises, all small, were Moore's IGA grocery, Arnold's Meat Locker, which sold only frozen meat, Lucas' Convenience Store, a barber shop, a post office and a branch of the Bank of Nova Scotia. On her first Sunday in Carp, Janet walked alone up the steep hill to St. Paul's United Church. She'd thought church might give her a chance to wear the outfits she'd brought from Hong Kong. She was wrong; the dress and hairstyles of the local farmers' wives had not even caught up to the fashions in old Hollywood movies.

More than anything, Janet's despair came from sheer loneliness. Neither her in-laws nor her husband engaged her in conversation. Once she had dared to ask if she could try cooking—she wanted to learn, and moreover she craved Chinese cuisine. Her in-laws wouldn't let her near the stove: "We can't trust you." They only spoke to her to lecture or complain about what she had or hadn't done.

Janet kept her sadness from her husband, and anyway, she didn't expect sympathy. Perversely, her isolation became valuable to her; she came to treasure, even guard it. She decided she would do what her in-laws asked of her and not talk back or utter a word of complaint. Neither would she speak to them unless they spoke to her first.

OF THE FORTY-FIVE YEARS that old Mr. Lang had lived in Canada, he had spent forty as a "married bachelor." He'd first left his village in 1910 to join an older brother in Vancouver who had lined up work for him as a cook for a doctor's family. He'd returned to China in 1915 to marry, and finally, eight years later, having repaid his brother for the expense of bringing him over, had saved enough to pay his wife's boat passage and head tax. He was too late: Mrs. Lang's steamship was mid-ocean when the Exclusion Act was passed, and when the ship came into port, Canadian authorities sent her back to China. At thirty-three, Mr. Lang, not yet a father, made the first of three visits to his wife before the war with Japan halted travel across the Pacific. Each of those visits produced a child, the youngest of whom was Golden.

Over the years, Mr. Lang migrated east from Vancouver. By 1949, he was working at a coffee shop in Goderich, near Lake Huron in southern Ontario. Then a friend asked him to help out at his café on the Quebec side of the Ottawa River. After a stint at the Royal Café in Campbell's Bay, a couple of hours upriver from Ottawa, he moved ten miles farther to Fort Coulonge, to the Coulonge Café. One of the partners, Lem Howe, asked Mr. Lang to replace him while he went to Hong Kong to look for a wife. From Fort Coulonge, Mr. Lang and Mr. Howe's partner, Joe Lee, began the process of bringing their families from China. Mr. Lee applied for his wife (a cousin of Mr. Lang); and Mr. Lang for his wife and Golden.

The first to arrive in Fort Coulonge were Golden and Mr. Howe and his new wife.

Golden had no memory of his father, whose last visit to China had ended when he was only a baby. The teenager saw that if he didn't quickly learn English, he'd have only his father's adult friends to speak to, a prospect he didn't relish. One of the first locals he met was the Anglican minister, Monsieur Emard, who took his supper at the café while waiting for the Ottawa train with the daily mail, which he would distribute to his parishioners in Yarm, Stark's Corners, Charteris, Shawville and Otter Lake. Seeing the tedium of Golden's eleven-hour days at the café, the minister took the young man under his wing and extended an invitation to visit him and his wife. When he saw Golden's face light up at his collection of black and white photographs, the minister offered to teach him how to take pictures and develop them.

Within a year, Messrs Lang, Howe and Lee all had their wives in Canada, and the three families shared the living space above the Coulonge Café. The Howes were also expecting their first child. Mr. Lang knew it was time to move on again. The café could hardly support two families, never mind three. The next time Gerry Finer, who serviced nickelodeons in cafés around the area, showed up, he asked, "You know of any cafés for sale? In a small town?" He knew of only one. "Keith McMurtchy runs a lunch and gas bar in Carp; he wants out of the business." Lem Howe, whose English was better than Mr. Lang's, travelled with him to Carp to negotiate the purchase. He and Mr. McMurtchy settled on thirteen thousand dollars; Mr. Lang, superstitious about an unlucky number, deducted one dollar from the price.

Carp was a village of farmers where Armstrong was the most common name on the mailboxes. The village's first and only Chinese family for as long as they would remain there, the Langs had a cultural divide of their own. Just as Mr. Lang had lived most of his and his wife's marriage on his own in Canada, Mrs. Lang had lived akin to a widow in China. She'd raised three children on her own, two of whom were left behind in China and whom her husband hardly knew. With their reunion, Mr. and Mrs. Lang were resuming a marriage in its waning years, and reuniting as parents of their youngest child, who was already on the brink of adulthood. Their only shared experience was rooted in the mores of old China.

As for their son, Golden, he was capturing images of his own new reality, that of the present. When the Langs moved to Carp, he'd bought himself a Brownie camera. He set up developing equipment in the family bathroom, and would shut the door tight when he was at work. Into this company of strangers stepped Janet.

WHEN JANET WAS STILL a newlywed, her mother-in-law had crudely grabbed her ankle, shaking it like a loose table leg. "So skinny, just like Mrs. Lee said. You won't be giving birth to any babies."

Janet felt wounded; Mrs. Lee, whom she'd met once, had seemed so friendly.

"She got a good look at you, walking up her staircase."

On that particular day, Golden had a friend take the two of them on an outing so that he could show Janet the two cafés where his father had worked and where he and his mother had first lived when they came to Canada. The day had been a picturesque tour through some mill towns along the river, ending up in Fort Coulonge, originally a Hudson's Bay Company trading post. At the café there, Janet had accepted Mrs. Lee's invitation to tour the living quarters on the second floor. Now Janet realized that the café owner's wife clearly had her own eyes elsewhere.

By her second miscarriage, Janet began to think her mother-in-law was right. Maybe her ninety-four pounds were too slight to carry a baby to term. She had lost the first baby at six months along, the second at four months.

Now she was pregnant for the third time in less than three years of marriage. Dr. Daykin, Carp's only doctor, whom she saw in his home office up the street, said he would schedule her for monthly injections of synthetic hormones, which he hoped would prevent a miscarriage. But he was firm that Janet had to do her part: "Go home and relax, put your feet up. Get lots of sleep and rest."

This time, Janet felt it necessary to speak to her mother-in-law, to tell her what the doctor had advised. Mrs. Lang's response was swift: "Work still has to get done. Okay, you're pregnant, but until a baby comes, everybody has to work."

THE HIGHWAYS OF NORTHERN Ontario linked villages that had their heyday in the lumber trade at the turn of the century. Now, as before, they also brought travellers seeking the amenities of Ottawa. In this way, Highway 60 introduced old Mr. Lang to Mr. Tam, who ran a café 125 miles from Ottawa in the village of Barry's Bay, on the shores of Kamaniskeg Lake near Algonquin Park. The two men had first met when Mr. Tam, on his way to Ottawa, had stopped in at the Golden Café. Later, Mr. Tam invited the Langs to the wedding and reception of his son and a girl from Hong Kong. He also invited Janet and Golden, as he wanted Golden to take pictures.

On the wedding day, the Tams' chartered bus collected guests en route, ending up at Ottawa's Cathay House restaurant, the only place large enough to accommodate a banquet. Bill Joe, a son of the laundryman Shung Joe, had taken over ownership and management from its original sixteen shareholders. He had not only expanded the restaurant but added a second kitchen dedicated to the Chinese food on the menu and headed by an expert chef from Montreal.

One day, to Janet's surprise, the Tams' new daughter-in-law showed up in a highly agitated state at their door in Carp. Janet was alone; the others were on the café side. The girl had hitched a ride on a transport. The truckers all knew "Goldie's place": on any given night, as many as five or six drivers chose the Langs' lot as the place to park their rigs and catch a few hours' sleep.

The girl said life was so unbearable with her mother-in-law that she'd tried to kill herself by walking into the lake. She pleaded with Janet: "Help me buy a bus ticket to Vancouver." She had an uncle there who would take her in.

Janet was wide-eyed. "I don't know where to buy a ticket, or even how to buy one." The girl explained that it was money she needed; she had only the tips she'd earned in her father-in-law's café.

At this point, Mr. Lang came through the doorway from the kitchen.

The girl was bemoaning how she felt like a prisoner. She said Mrs. Tam was holding her Hong Kong passport and the jade and gold jewellery that she'd brought with her to Canada. And, she confessed, she was pregnant: "If I don't escape now, how will I be able to after the baby is born?"

Mr. Lang was outraged. "You cannot run away! Chinese people never do such things!" He dialled the café in Barry's Bay and spoke to Mr. Tam, who immediately sent his son down to Carp to collect his runaway wife. Janet later heard that the next day, the girl had to be restrained again from throwing herself into the lake.

As her third pregnancy advanced, Janet sought out a neighbour, Greta Armstrong, who had a one-year-old. The language barrier meant they didn't get far in conversation, but Janet was interested in learning how to knit. She wanted to have two sets of baby outfits ready. Between Greta and Lillian Reid, who delivered the mail and whose husband drove the Canada Bread truck, Janet was also introduced to quilting and pie-making.

One day in her seventh month, Janet had to make a dash to the toilet. She had passed blood. By the time Dr. Daykin arrived, she was already pushing. He was just in time to preside over the birth of a five-pound baby girl. Clifford Cox obliged with his car and delivered mother and baby to the hospital, half an hour away, in Arnprior. After a week in the incubator, the baby was ready to go home.

Janet's crying bouts ended with Arlene's birth, as she now had somebody other than herself to talk to. In time the toddler was charting an indiscriminate course between the living quarters and the café and Janet began to relinquish some of her isolation. When she'd come upon her mother-in-law in conversation with her husband, she would interject: "Is there news?" She persisted, even though Mrs. Lang always gave her the brush-off, telling her it was none of her business.

Janet found her own ways to get news. She read the weekly Chinese newspaper from Toronto that Mr. Lang subscribed to. She made a concerted effort to read the daily *Ottawa Journal* and the weekly *Carp Review*. She'd been excited when Mr. Lang bought a radio, thinking it would speed her learning of English, but to her disappointment, he kept it on the café side to provide music for the customers.

Determined, Janet worked on her English by listening to customers, and eventually, venturing small talk with the neighbourhood regulars. She knew she'd made progress when she could understand the teasing between Clifford Cox and her father-in-law. Clifford would start to talk insurance, and Mr. Lang, after humouring him briefly, would arbitrarily declare the start of Chinese New Year: "Chinese don't like to talk about death in the new year!"

Janet became matter-of-fact about the strain of life with her in-laws. These are not bad people, she thought. We're not really warring with each other; we just don't have much in common.

BY 1965, A DECADE INTO their marriage, Janet and Golden had three children, Arlene, Pearl and David, aged seven, five and two, and Janet was expecting again. That same year, the household suffered a blow that affected the rhythm of daily life much more than the arrival of any baby. Old Mr. Lang suddenly fell ill. For once, Golden, the new owner of a used car, a 1961 Plymouth that he'd bought cheap because it had suspect brakes, didn't have to rely on a neighbour in a medical emergency. He drove his father to the Arnprior hospital, but a couple of days later, the older man succumbed. The business of running the café left little time for mourning, as the work of four now fell on three.

One day early in her seventh month, Janet's water broke and, feeling the immediate onset of labour, she told Golden there was no time to drive her to the hospital. Call Dr. Daykin, she said. Tell him to come to the house. Sweating profusely, she lay down on their bed.

Given Janet's experience with Pearl, Dr. Daykin admitted her to the hospital early with David. Her only memory of Pearl's birth was a sudden feeling of cold, then of standing on a cloud. She came to at the sound of a nurse's voice: "You awake? You were in real danger there for a while!" But David had been a full-term baby and his delivery uneventful.

Old Mrs. Lang came into the bedroom. "The doctor hasn't come yet?" Not seeing him, she left. Janet considered her mother-in-law's behaviour to be predictable, worrying less about her daughter-in-law being in labour than about keeping her son away until the baby was born.

Left on her own, Janet finally could no longer fight the urge to push.

The baby slid out, face down.

Waiting for a cry and hearing none, Janet panicked. With as much energy as she could muster, she called out: "Help, help!"

Mrs. Lang returned.

"Turn the baby over," Janet whimpered. "Hurry."

The old lady approached, then recoiled: "It's so dirty. Dirty and slimy!" While Mrs. Lang willingly, even happily, minded her three grandchildren, she refused to change a single diaper. Now she strode out of the room.

Janet struggled to sit up. She reached and grasped the baby's bottom, but the baby squirted away from her. She reached again, but it only slid farther. On her third try, the baby slipped off the end of the bed. She prayed: If this baby lives, it will be God's doing. Good luck to us all.

Suddenly the baby let out a cry. Dr. Daykin arrived and when he discovered that Janet had delivered the baby on her own, he shook his head. "You both were lucky," he said.

Janet thought something else ought to be remembered about Peter's birth—that he was the first Chinese boy to be born in Carp. David, after all, was born in Arnprior. Janet would take ownership of other memories in her life. When her daughters, Arlene and Pearl, were old enough to play dress-up, she went into her closet, collected the high-heeled shoes she'd packed from Hong Hong and never worn, and let the girls play with them. Might as well get some enjoyment from them; one could hardly walk around in heels carrying a pot of hot coffee or pumping gas.

WHEN ARLENE WAS A YEAR from starting high school, Golden and Janet decided they ought to make a move to Ottawa. Carp finally had a new elementary school, built two years earlier to commemorate Canada's hundredth birthday, but high school students still had to be bussed to Arnprior.

Also influencing Golden's decision was his sense that the family business held no future for his children. Keeping the café had become more onerous with just three adults, one of them an aging grandmother, and the other two, a busy mother and a father who also held down a part-time job. Golden had parlayed his photography hobby into work making offset plates for the *Carp Review.*

In fact, Golden wanted to try his hand at making a living from photo finishing. The Eastman Kodak company had recently introduced colour film, which was growing in popularity among professional photographers, including the portrait and wedding photographer favoured by Ottawa's Chinese community, Tsin Van, a Chinese national who had settled in town. Inconveniently for Ottawa-based photographers, the nearest processing facility for colour film was in Toronto. Seeing an opportunity, Golden offered colour processing and, in order to attract clients, provided pickup and delivery service. He traded his aged Plymouth for a more reliable used car. As his client base grew, he remembered what his father had said when he made the move to Carp: "The money won't come to you; you have to go to the money."

So Golden and Janet purchased a modest postwar house in Ottawa on busy Carling Avenue, one of the city's main west–east arteries. At the same time as they were selling the café and preparing to move, Janet received unexpected news. Her parents had immigrated to New York City, taking with them her two young brothers but leaving her married sisters behind in Hong Kong. They said they wanted to visit Canada. One of the first things she would stock her new kitchen with, Janet decided, was a set of cookbooks. Already, she imagined the spread she would put on for her visiting family, and equally, the disbelief on their faces.

Three generations—Golden's mother, the couple and their four children—moved in to the Langs' new house in Ottawa. Golden decided to set up his business, "Golden Colour Lab," in the basement. Upstairs, in the living room, on the upper shelf of a built-in bookcase, Janet carefully placed *Fook, Luk, Sau,* the set of three figurines she'd brought with her so many years ago from Hong Kong.

Lai-sim Leung and her son, Billy, her grandfather,
Harry Yee, and Chun Yee (wife of Lai-sim's brother, Henry)
in front of Harry's Café and Confectionery, Altona, Manitoba.

TEN

LIVES

ONE CAN IMAGINE, for a moment, the process of immigration as similar to passage through a sieve that separates two worlds, the homeland from the new world. The family begins with the weight of yearning for a better life and hopes to be left with the essential attributes of success. For many Chinese who immigrated from China or Hong Kong after Canada lifted exclusion, life abroad seemed like an exile, so isolating that they had to keep reminding themselves why they'd come. Adding to the stress of living abroad, the terms by which they'd entered Canada—as sponsored family members or fiancées—worked to both unite and to separate families. To borrow another analogy from the kitchen, sending a family member abroad was like separating an egg white from the yolk. It allowed a family to treat its parts in different ways, but in its memory, they were still one.

THE MOMENT HIS FRIEND, visiting Hong Kong from Ottawa, departed, the eldest son of the Ha family took out pen and paper to compose a letter to his sister.

He had asked his visitor about this sister, Kwok-chun, or by her Christian name, Marion. Eldest Brother had not seen her in five years, since her marriage in 1958 to the restaurateur Tom-yee Hum of Ottawa. Knowing that Ottawa's Chinese community was small, he was sure his friend, even if he hadn't seen her, would have heard something.

Eldest Brother had raised his younger siblings, and though they were now adults, he still took that responsibility to heart. He'd accepted that role when their father, with their mother barely in the grave, stunned his children by announcing that he had a second wife and other young children and that he would be moving them in. Together with the older siblings, Eldest Brother had refused to allow another woman into what had been their mother's domain. As a consequence, their father, not a man to argue or raise his voice, disappeared from their lives.

The third youngest of eleven children—of which seven survived infancy—Marion Ha was nine when she lost, in effect, both parents. A beauty with classic almond-shaped eyes and an assertive personality, evident even when young, Marion had had many admirers in Hong Kong but had married the first man she dated. While Eldest Brother personally knew of Tom Hum, he'd been concerned about his sister moving to Canada, where she'd be without family.

In Ottawa, Marion Hum opened her brother's letter and was amused to read of gossip having travelled so far, of her reportedly looking "alarmingly thin." That it worried her brother was obvious in the scrawl of his handwriting across the page.

"Don't tell me your husband has another wife," he wrote. "Or that he already had one before you, that you're a second wife. If that's the case, come back to Hong Kong."

So, my brother fears the worst, thought Marion, that the infidelity our mother had to contend with has now befallen me.

Only a hint of her father's presence had remained with her, a memory of his hand brushing the top of her head. In contrast, especially since Marion had begun her married life in Ottawa, the voice of her mother, which ran deeper than memory, played over and again in her mind.

"No matter what happens to you, don't cry."

In the months of her mother's illness with cancer—which at the time she kept hidden from her family, dismissing it as a chronic "stomach ache"—young Marion preferred sitting in a little chair by her mother's sickbed to playing with her siblings. At the funeral, when she'd cried so hard that her body cramped up to the tips of her fingers and toes, she'd remembered her mother's prescient words. She would later reflect that her mother must have realized how terribly this particular child would miss her when she was gone.

She knew that Eldest Brother wished only for her happiness. Even as she and Tom were about to leave for Canada, he'd taken her aside, to remind her yet again that if she wasn't happy there, she was to write him and he'd find the money for airfare to bring her home.

Marion felt she couldn't confess to her brother what she had unwittingly got herself into in Ottawa. If she thought its airport terminal looked as welcoming as a warehouse, she was in for a greater disillusion when she saw her marital home. The house that Tom owned with a younger brother—it had been his idea to buy it because he feared his brother and wife and two children might have trouble finding a landlord to rent to them—turned out to be premises shared with a dozen bachelor tenants. His brother's family had the ground floor. Tom and Marion moved into two rooms on the second floor, and the bachelors occupied the remaining rooms on their floor and in the attic.

Any expectation Marion might have had that her sister-in-law would be good company was quickly dispelled. The prickly woman preferred to spend her time tending a tiny backyard plot where she grew Chinese vegetables. She said the garden helped to lessen her homesickness for the life in her village in China.

Left to herself, Marion felt wrenched from the active life she'd enjoyed in Hong Kong. Ottawa had no Chinese cinema, no Chinese language television programs, no Chinese book-stores, or newspapers or magazines. Nor did Marion have enough comprehension of English to read the Ottawa dailies; she had to rely on Tom to tell her the news. But he had no time; he worked seven days a week at his restaurant, the Lucky Key. Their social life was non-existent. They didn't even dine at his restaurant. Tom said he'd have to pay in his own estab-lishment to set the right example for his partners. But he also ruled out their dining at *any* restaurant in town: "That would be like saying my own food isn't good enough to eat."

In any event, within two months of their wedding in Hong Kong and one month of arriving in Ottawa, Marion became pregnant. I'm stuck here now, she told herself. She started having babies as fast as nature allowed: Victor was born that winter. When he was only a few months old, she was pregnant a second time, with Wallace. Hardly had he arrived when for the third time in little more than three years, she was pregnant again, with Debbie, who was born prematurely.

Marion considered how to reply to the letter from her brother. She told him he could put his mind at ease; he was reading too much into her weight loss: "I'm busy that's all—I keep having babies!" She kept the tone light, asking him to send her some best-quality dried Chinese mushrooms and rice noodles; she missed the ones as fine as silk thread, that soften within seconds of being immersed in cold water.

If Marion had written honestly of her feelings about life in Canada, she would have said that she was a prisoner of boredom. *I feel as if I'm locked up*, she'd told herself. Her days passed in monotony. The weekly shop for groceries was the only time she got out of the house—but even then, especially in winter, she had to force herself. Once a week she made the effort of dressing the children, getting them down the stairs and the little ones into the pram, and making the long walk from their house on Lisgar to Bank Street, to the IGA grocery store. The public health unit where she took the children for their immunizations was nearby, so it was a route she knew well. Then it was back to the house, a mile and a half in all. Rarely could she muster the enthusiasm to walk with the children in the other direction, up to Albert Street to pick up something from the Chinese confectionery there. Apart from the extra three blocks' walk each way, she didn't think it worth going because the selection was limited and the quality poor, the exception being the cured Chinese sausages that came from Montreal.

No matter what happens to you, don't cry. Marion was not going to cry. But if she did, she told herself, it would be because precisely nothing happened. Certainly her life didn't measure up to her Chinese name, which combined the character for "heroine" with that for "valuable." Yet how prophetic the choice of her Christian name. Her sister had suggested

Marion, inspired by the calypso song on everybody's lips at the time:

All night, all day, Marianne
Down by the seaside siftin' sand

That, Marion decided, was her sentence: sifting the sands of time, her days shaped only by babies and children. If something doesn't change, she told herself, I'm going to go crazy.

LIFE HERE IS WORSE THAN JAIL, eighteen-year-old Henry Yee told himself.

When one of the boys on the football field would hand off the football to him, he'd run and run, sometimes right past the end zone. He would hear the boys yelling at him, "Stop!" but he couldn't stop. He'd imagine himself running straight out of Altona, one deke right past fields where Holstein and Shorthorn cattle grazed, one deke left past fields of swaying grain, then straight on some seventy miles, and he'd be in the big city of Winnipeg, giving his grandfather the slip, so he wouldn't have to put up with his nagging any more.

"He gives me hell and shit all the time. Every minute!" Henry complained to Earl Dick, the teenaged son of the owner of the garage and car dealership next door to his grandfather's business, Harry's Café and Confectionery. He confided the same to Earl's father. "He's not a happy person. No matter what I do, I can't please him."

From afar, in Hong Kong, Henry had understood that his grandfather was getting old, feeling the ache in his bones, and lamenting the hard work of his café and store. When Canada announced the end of exclusion, Henry's father had written to him: "*Baba,* I'm too old to come to Canada; do you want to get my son over to help you?"

That was three years ago.

His grandfather's establishment, on one half a counter with seven booths and on the other, grocery shelves with a meat box in the middle, was a seven-day-a-week concern. Grandfather Harry did the cooking and baking. Other than the young boy who washed dishes, a white middle-aged waitress was the only paid staff. Henry had to work both sides of the business. Often he could be run off his feet: he'd have a customer in the café, another at the meat box waiting to make a selection, which he had to wrap, weigh and price, and customers from both sides lined up at the cash. In any lull, Henry was expected to keep the grocery shelves stocked— mostly canned tomatoes, carrots, peas and green beans. Plus, twice a week when the restaurant took delivery of meat from Canada Packers, he had to help his grandfather cut it up for display.

Of all the days of the week, Henry most dreaded Sundays, for everybody else, a day of rest. For him, a fifteen-hour work day lay ahead. In addition to minding the café and store, he also had to mop, clean and wipe down everything, from the floor to the shelves, the booths to the meat box. Henry took to secretly hiring the dishwasher to help him. For twenty-five cents, the boy was willing to come in early to wash the floor. Henry left his bedroom window open and a rope dangling, with one end attached to his toe, as he slept on a mattress on the floor. The boy's tug signalled him to rise and quietly let him in; a knock at that hour would wake his grandfather.

Henry had no complaint about hard work, only resentment at having no free time. His grandfather took time off to bowl and curl; Henry figured he deserved the same. But when he did decide to join friends, to play football, shoot pool, or hunt rabbits at someone's farm, the moment he walked back in the door the old man would be on his case; he didn't think "play" was good for building a young man's character.

Perhaps owing to Altona's history as a close-knit Mennonite community, Henry's friends and their parents took no sides between the old man and the boy. When he'd arrived in town, everyone clamoured for a first sighting of "the Chinese boy," his arrival doubling the town's Chinese population. For the fifteen months that Henry attended school, enthusiastic children from kindergarten up vied to be the one to hold up English vocabulary flashcards for the gregarious boy with the large innocent eyes. They were amused at his first English words: O'Henry (Harry Yee said that he'd assigned his grandson the name Henry after his best-selling candy bar), hamburger, hot dog, french fries, pork chops, strawberry short cake—all items on the café's menu.

Despite people's good intentions, it got so that Henry began to feel that the whole town was on him too. If it wasn't "Henry, your grandfather needs you," it was "Henry, can you help your grandfather? You know he can't walk anymore." Even corns on one's feet counted as public knowledge in such a small town.

One glorious summer's day, Henry got a hankering to join friends for a swim at a nearby lake. He took the keys to his grandfather's 1949 Ford Meteor, which the old man had bought new, and headed down the road. He skidded on the gravel, sending the car glancing off a tree and smashing the windshield. Of course, when he got home, despite his gashed and bloodied cheek, he got an earful from his exasperated grandfather. Not long after that, Henry decided to run away. A day later, a neighbour from Altona, dispatched by his old man, found him in Winnipeg. "Henry, your grandfather wants you to come back; he says he won't give you shit no more." Within two weeks, the old man was back to his nagging ways.

He only wants me here to work, Henry concluded.

Nineteen was too old to be living under your grandfather's thumb. The next time, Henry didn't run away; he said goodbye and left for Winnipeg. Neither his grandfather nor anyone else from Altona bothered to come after him.

GIVEN THE CHANCE, it would be smart to get out of Hong Kong, thought Marion Ha. The combination of marriage and Canada, she decided, was that chance.

Since she was young, it had been Marion's ambition to study hard, get high marks and land a good job. She credited her scholarly mother, whose father sent her brothers to school but, unusual for the time, hired a private tutor for his daughter. Marion's mother went on to become a teacher in the village. At home, she demanded extra from her children. Each had to produce five hundred characters daily for her approval. Later, as a student in Hong Kong, Marion supplemented what she considered to be the poor quality of the school in the colony by becoming a voracious reader, just as happy to read Chinese classics as translations of *Jane Eyre* or *Pride and Prejudice*.

The absence of a mother had made Marion determined to face life with purpose: one had to set a goal, make a plan and act on it. Such was her mother's strength, to which the Ha children attributed their very survival. She had uprooted the family twice. When the Japanese spilled over China's northern border, she first moved them from the village to Canton, where their father worked as a high-ranking employee of a French-owned bank. Previously, they saw him only when he came home on weekends. That move saved the family from Japanese bombers and soldier patrols. To protect its banking industry, Canton sheltered bankers in its foreign concession, which remained free from Japanese attack; such concessions were home to expatriates from some of Japan's Second World War allies, or from countries like France that had surrendered to Germany.

Their mother's second move came at war's end. Rather than return to their village, she decided to re-establish herself and the children in Hong Kong, leaving her husband to travel from Canton to the colony on weekends. She'd intended to use the cache of American dollars and jewellery she'd brought to Hong Kong to invest in property, to provide an income for herself and the children. But illness struck before she could do so. Within the year, she was dead. When the children lost their father to his second wife, they'd lived off that money and jewellery until the older siblings could find work. When the Communists took over China, the children, relieved to be safe in Hong Kong, thanked their mother yet again for her foresight.

Single-minded about coming first in her classes, Marion had remained oblivious to boys and romance; only after the fact did she realize she'd been asked on a date. A boy suggested he could take her to a movie, to which she had answered with indignation: "What for? I have my own money if I want to go!" But by the time she was working as a reporter for *Wah Kiu Yat Pao,* one of the colony's two Chinese dailies, Marion was well aware of Hong Kong's status as a bride market. The personal classifieds placed by men in Canada seeking a wife were increasingly popular.

In Marion's opinion, it was folly to meet blind, by way of an advertisement; better that an introduction be made. So when a friend of her brother's asked if she'd be a pen pal to Tom Hum, a good friend of his in Canada, she'd already warmed to the idea of an overseas friendship. And so the two began a correspondence. After some months, Tom hinted at a more serious relationship. He'd just opened a new restaurant, which he'd have to work hard at to get it established: "Can you wait a few years for me?" The bluntness of Marion's reply—"Sorry, you go your way, I'll go mine"—brought Tom to Hong Kong to woo her. He'd taken six months off, the most he felt he could afford to be away. Marion expected she'd have to decide quickly about marrying Tom, if only because it was too much to ask him to pay another airfare to return for a wedding. Sure enough, he proposed, suggesting that the two marry in Hong Kong and he'd send for her at a later date. But Marion was adamant: "If you leave me behind, I will not marry you."

The two wed at Hong Kong's city hall. Marion was twenty-one; Tom was thirty-one. She had yet to meet any of his family. She knew that the Hum name was well respected in Ottawa. In 1897, Tom's grandfather, Mong Hum, and his brother, Kwong, both laundrymen, became the first Chinese in the city to take out their naturalization papers. In 1925,

the brothers, who at that time owned the Wing On confectionery on Albert Street, got together with laundryman
Shung Joe, and Sue Wong, the grocer at the Yick Lung store,
and purchased forty plots at Beechwood Cemetery, to be
reserved for bachelor men who died destitute and without
next-of-kin, thereby establishing a Chinese section of the
cemetery. Had it not been for exclusion, Tom, born in China,
would have been a third-generation Canadian. But in the
eight years since he emigrated to Canada in 1949, he went
from waiting on tables at the Ding Ho Café (downstairs
from the Wing On) to opening the Lucky Key restaurant in
an Ottawa suburb.

Canada had tipped Marion's decision in Tom's favour. In
the years of trying to make sense of her parents' marriage,
what she'd learned had soured her on life as a married woman
in Hong Kong. She'd come to a verdict on the island colony.
If you're someone who is poor here, she decided, you work
hard for the rich. If you're rich, then you keep a second wife
or a mistress, or both.

Marion learned that her mother and her older siblings had
long known about her father's philandering. By her siblings'
account, they'd asked their mother why she didn't have it out
with their father. Her reply had been matter-of-fact: "Your
father is a man who loves women. If we argued and he didn't
come home, where would I go, with so many children?" She
went so far as to defend him, praising him for keeping his
affairs outside the home, and without fail, returning on weekends to their marital bed.

When Marion and Tom had first begun to write to each
other, they exchanged photographs. Contemplating the image

of the slight man, with his hair precisely parted and a shy, even worried expression, Marion told herself, this is the face of an honest man. The kind who would keep a wife, who wouldn't look at another woman—not like my father.

IN WINNIPEG, Henry fell in with the wrong crowd, gambling for the first time in his life. He had arrived knowing nobody, and before long, whatever he earned he mostly left behind at the gambling clubs. He drifted from job to job, working the kitchens of Chinese-owned cafés or waiting on tables in coffee shops. Four years passed in this way.

One day, while behind the counter at the Exchange Café, Henry received a surprise telephone call from his brother-in-law. Gordon Lee had arrived at the train station. He'd flown from Hong Kong to Vancouver, then boarded the train to Winnipeg. He was on his way to Altona, to work for Henry's grandfather, and wanted to meet for coffee.

Like Henry, Gordon had entered the country as a paper son. He had engaged in a further deception, that he was single; Canada's rules allowed sponsorship only of unmarried dependents.

Henry and Gordon had last seen each other a decade ago in Hong Kong, when Gordon and Henry's older sister had wed.

As he expected, Henry got a scolding from his brother-in-law, about the family having heard little or nothing from him since he'd left Altona. He didn't mean letters; since Henry couldn't write Chinese, no one expected a letter. Rather, he meant remittances. Regular at first—Henry had sent home thirty out of the forty dollars he earned each month—they'd become sporadic, then stopped altogether.

"We wondered if you were dead."

"I've been a bad guy." Henry confessed; he'd got into a habit of gambling. "If I win, I send money. If I lose, I don't."

That matter settled, Gordon announced that he had "big news" for Henry.

Henry couldn't think what family news, good or bad, would affect his feelings one way or another. His obligations to help support them aside, he felt no emotional attachment to any of them. Of his birth family, he had only his father and two sisters. His father's attentions had long ago been elsewhere: he'd recently remarried, to a girl young enough to be his daughter, and was raising a second family of three children. His eldest sister had married Gordon, and thus was "gone out." His youngest sister had been adopted out when she was three years old and no one had spoken of her since. He had no idea of her fate.

"Your little sister is married and living in Ottawa."

Henry was speechless when he heard that news. The middle child of three, he was five when he'd last seen her. The three siblings had just lost their mother. The family, thinking they were protecting his feelings, told him a lie, that his mother was sick and gone for a few days when in fact she had died. Soon after that, his grandmother took away his little sister, Lai-sim, and returned home without her, producing in her stead a sack of rice and some sausages.

Gordon told Henry that Lai-sim had been trying to track him down. She'd written to their grandfather in Altona, but the old man had thrown out her letters, with the excuse that he couldn't read Chinese.

Although Henry had been working a scant two months

at the Exchange Café, the owner obliged by granting him the month off he asked for to visit his sister in Ottawa. Henry had never been east of Winnipeg, but he felt like he was going home.

"WE NEED OUR OWN PLACE." Marion tried to persuade Tom that four years of living with his brother was enough, that they ought to buy their own home. He was hesitant, wondering how his brother would fare and not wanting to leave him and his family on their own.

"Don't worry," said Marion.

The Lucky Key restaurant was doing well, helped by its prime location opposite the entrance to busy Westgate Shopping Centre, the city's first, on Carling Avenue. Tom found a bungalow on Fisher Avenue not far from the restaurant, in the suburb of Queensboro (later renamed Westboro). Marion's conversations with neighbours helped to improve her English and she learned to drive.

Yet again, Marion saw Tom and herself as the perfect match: where he could see detail, she could see the big picture. Where he was timid, she was brave. Without courage, she often reminded him, you can't have success.

HENRY AND LAI-SIM looked and sounded like siblings: both stocky and round-shouldered and prone to a slight chubbiness, both with an almost identical timbre to their voices that could convey, with equal depth, sorrow or joy. Both wept freely at the sight of each other. Lai-sim had no memory of Henry; he told of how he used to carry her around their village, strapped to his back.

The two visited in her home, in the two small upstairs rooms that Lai-sim and her husband, Yu-nam Leung, and their baby, Billy, rented in the rooming house on Frank Street.

The siblings had been separated for twenty years, yet so much of their lives in that time had followed the same trajectory. Both had lost the only mother they'd known. Both had been raised by grandparents, Henry by a grandmother gone nearly blind, who'd lived her entire married life separated from her husband in Canada; Lai-sim by her surviving adoptive grandfather. Both had fled their villages after Liberation, escaping to Hong Kong.

Their grandfather's life abroad had begun decades before in Timmins, in northern Ontario, and eventually, led to Altona. After Liberation, Harry Yee had urged his extended household of nine, including adults and children, to escape to Hong Kong: "I will support you all." Within months, Harry was no longer on his own; his grandson, Henry, arrived in Canada to work alongside him.

By the time the stranger smuggled Lai-sim, with nothing but the clothes on her back and sandals of dried citrus peel on her feet, to the border of Hong Kong to meet her birth father, Henry had Altona in his rear-view mirror, and was about to slide into an idle life of gambling in Winnipeg. He explained to his sister why he'd left his grandfather: "I had a bed, I had food; I couldn't complain, but I didn't feel he cared about me."

Lai-sim shared the same sentiment about her life in Hong Kong, before she was dispatched to Canada as a bride to Yu-nam. A relative of the family in Hong Kong had shamed Grandfather Harry's wife into taking her back into the family: "You eat well, but you leave your poor granddaughter in

China to starve?" In Hong Kong, when Lai-sim wasn't at her factory job, sewing children's clothes and cowboy pants, she was expected to babysit her half-siblings and cousins and to clean house. But she too felt unloved: "Grandmother and Second Mother were superstitious about a girl coming back into the family; they thought I might bring bad luck."

In their month together, the two siblings shed as many tears in laughter as in sorrow. Lai-sim told of having arrived in Ottawa in the dead of winter, thinking the whiteness to be sand. She wondered why people didn't chop down the bony leafless trees for firewood, only to be astonished the following spring to see them turn green. Henry said in Altona the overnight snowdrifts could pile so high against the door of the restaurant as to trap him and his grandfather inside. He'd have to crank the phone to call a neighbour for help.

"Don't go back to Winnipeg. Come and live with me," Lai-sim begged her brother. "I can't speak English; you could translate for me." Henry decided to do the honourable thing by his boss at the Exchange Café: go back to work and give him two months' notice.

IN THE FALL OF 1964, Marion Hum, still new to the game of mahjong, told her newfound friends that her baby, her fourth, due in December, would keep her away for a while. They understood; when a mother has young babies, she has no time.

In Hong Kong, Marion's older siblings had all played mahjong—they'd had a couple of sets at home—but she had studiously avoided the game, preferring to pore over her books. But one day in Ottawa, a woman she'd met through one of the wives of Tom's partners invited her to her house, offering to teach her the game. Marion accepted. My life is so dull, why not? she said to herself. She'd joined in a couple times, taken the bus across town, the stop on Bank Street where she should alight easily identifiable by the landmark of the Colonial Furniture store. From there, it was a short walk to the woman's house on James Street.

Among those new acquaintances around the mahjong table, Marion met Lai-sim Leung. She traced the beginning of their friendship to several weeks later, during her stay in hospital when she gave birth to Lynda. As it happened Lai-sim had a friend also in hospital, and she came twice a day to deliver a hot meal of rice to her.

Marion and Lai-sim promised to see each other again over mahjong. Lai-sim said she had two others who could make up a foursome: Chun, the wife of her brother, Henry, who shared their house, and as well, Lui-sang Wong, who lived just steps away on the same street. Marion knew of Lui-sang, who was known to her husband. When Tom had been in Hong Kong courting her, as a favour to Lui-sang's paper family, also of the surname Hum, he'd escorted the young teenager she was then to Canadian Immigration for her interview.

Of course, said Lai-sim, all of us are busy mothers, still having babies, with no time. And for now, she was also holding down a job washing dishes, in order to keep up her remittances to her family in Hong Kong. She said Lui-sang had a big house, with a large second-floor veranda, an enjoyable place on a summer's evening and big enough for a card table. Maybe one day, she could host a game. Marion said she could be counted on to come back to the game. "I'd have gone mad," she said, "if I hadn't learned to play mahjong."

More than that, all the pairs of hands shuffling the tiles, reaching for them, stacking them, and then starting anew, was not just comforting, but like a kind of life force. Lai-sim already had in mind a name for the mothers who could come together over a mahjong date: the sisterhood.

Marion Lim, on the runway modelling
T. Eaton Company's spring fashions, 1958.
Courtesy Marion Lew

ELEVEN

HOME

MARION LIM TOOK THE bus to the foot of Burrard Street, to the Marine Building, the Art Deco skyscraper on Vancouver's waterfront. She stepped off the elevator at the floor for the Faulkner-Smith School of Applied and Fine Art and, once inside, asked for Mr. Howard Faulkner-Smith.

The artist didn't know the teenaged girl: "What can I do for you?"

Marion introduced herself, saying that she'd seen his classified ad seeking a Chinese model.

Both the painter, now in his sixties, and his school, which prepared students for a career in commercial graphic arts, were well known. A graduate of a prestigious art academy in London, England, and the son of a baron, Mr. Faulkner-Smith had immigrated to Canada in his youth. He'd first exhibited his work in Vancouver thirty years earlier, in the 1920s. In the city's fledgling art culture of the time, patrons preferred landscapes such as his, rendered in watercolours, the trademark medium of English painters, to the work of a controversial new school of painters who called themselves the Group of Seven.

"You don't look Chinese." To Mr. Faulkner-Smith, the girl looked European.

Marion was used to this. Even in China, she'd hear people ask her mother: "Is this a girl your husband adopted from Canada?" The ambiguity of her looks came up again at her private school in Canton, where her classmates nicknamed her "Spanish." And in Canada, waiters in Chinatown sometimes ignored Marion, addressing themselves only to her Chinese friends.

She assured Mr. Faulkner-Smith that she was native to China. She was born Fay-oi Lim and had immigrated to Canada three years before, in 1950. "I'd like to model for you."

"Very well, since nobody has answered my ad," the artist said, grudgingly. "But, do you own a *cheong sam*?"

"Of course!" Marion replied. "I'm Chinese!"

AMONG MARION'S CLASSMATES at Vancouver Technical School, the goal upon graduation was a secretarial position. For a Chinese graduate, a bigger hurdle was landing a job outside Chinatown, and somewhere other than a Chinese-owned business.

The Canadian Parliament had extended the vote and other rights of citizenship to the Chinese in Canada by this time, but other barriers of discrimination would be slow to fall. Employers regularly turned away Chinese applicants with "We don't hire Chinese." An exception was businesses with a Chinese clientele. When Canadian Pacific Air Lines began flying between Hong Kong and Vancouver, it needed "greeters" at the airport. Arriving passengers had little idea that one of them was none other than the "Yo-yo King," Harvey Lowe. The voice of the weekly radio show "Call of Chinatown," broadcast on Vancouver's CJOR from the Bamboo Terrace nightclub, Harvey was best known for having won, at the age of thirteen, the first-ever yo-yo world championship, held in London, England. Jeanne Yuen, the friend of Marion's who could whip up a dress overnight, had Canadian Pacific as a client at the agency where she was a secretary—her job was to verify that applicants to the airline could speak Chinese as they claimed.

Marion's approach to securing her future remained unwavering: *Learn English, Marion. Learn English.* However discouraged she'd been when her father quashed her dream of going to university, she'd resolved to keep improving her language skills. Knowing that English would always be her second language, she was clear in her mind that when time came for marriage, she did not want a husband who was a recent immigrant like herself. *What if we had legal matters or documents to deal with? She wondered if both of us are immigrants, we'd be doubly handicapped; one of us should be able to communicate perfectly in English.* Better, she decided, that she marry someone Canadian-born.

One day, Marion was reading a local English daily newspaper and spied an advertisement for courses offered by the Elizabeth Leslie Fashion School. The Vancouver school was the second one opened by its founder, a finalist for the new Miss Canada pageant of 1948. The first, established the year after the competition, was in her hometown of Edmonton.

"For Modelling or for Personal Development," the ad said.

Personal development; that's for me. Marion suddenly thought about how she'd put all her effort into improving her ability in English, when obviously, comportment and self-assurance had just as much bearing on one's success as an immigrant. She had only to recall the disastrous night out at The Cave, when she and her date sat glum-faced through the entire evening.

Of the ten girls in the four-month course, held three evenings a week, Marion Lim was the only Chinese. Much to her surprise, at the end of the course, the school's director named her the top-ranked student. Each student had a photo shoot with John Gade, the city's only high-fashion photographer, so that they'd have a portfolio to launch their careers. What the school didn't say was that anyone serious about working in the fashion trade in Canada headed to Toronto, a city being transformed by postwar immigrants who'd lived in the great cities of Europe and brought their sophistication with them. The school's only advice was that if the girls expected to be paid to model, they needed to accumulate experience by volunteering as hostesses for local women's organizations, charities and community events. Eventually, the school might be able to add their names to its list of models that it referred for paying assignments.

MARION'S NEXT extracurricular course—she was still a high school student—was one in public speaking offered by the U.S.-based Dale Carnegie School, the originator of courses extolling "the power of self-improvement." As recommended by the fashion school, she also made volunteer appearances to build up her resumé, including modelling for Mr. Faulkner-Smith, who painted several large canvasses of her in her *cheong sam*. She received more charity requests than she had time for, since her father still expected her to help out at the coat and hat check at W.K. Gardens.

When she graduated from Vancouver Tech, Marion

decided to test whether an employer would be prepared to hire her as a model. She took her portfolio to Eaton's. The department store had come to British Columbia when it bought out the Spencer's chain in 1948. Mr. Milligan in the personnel department was enthusiastic about using Marion as a model, though he said Eaton's didn't have much work: "What we do is put you on the staff list for women's wear, and then when we have an assignment, we call you." And call her they did.

So began Marion's professional modelling career. As Eaton's made Marion's name, the photographer John Gade and the fashion school funnelled ever more assignments her way. A model in Vancouver could earn as much as a hundred dollars for a day's assignment, which was what Marion's former class-mates at Vancouver Tech working as secretaries could hope to make in a month. An evening assignment could earn her another seventy-five dollars. She became even busier when Eaton's took its fashion shows on the road around the prov-ince to show off *prêt-à-porter* wardrobes, sell the collections, bolster the store's image and reward devoted catalogue users. Always, Marion was the last model to walk down the runway, and in a show-stopping outfit.

From the start, Vancouver fashion writers gushed over Marion. "Vancouver's Own and North America's Most Beautiful Oriental Model," wrote one. Another described her as "exotically lovely" and a "China doll." Marion was the face of the Vancouver Eaton's "Touch of the Orient" collections and of Canadian Pacific Air Lines' "Fastest Routes to the Orient" advertising campaigns. In some of her more lucrative assignments, her lips advertised Max Factor lipsticks, and her smooth hands tempted the housewife to buy the newest convenience of domesticity, the automatic dishwasher.

MARION FUMBLED FOR the phone. She'd worked long hours the day before, with a modelling assignment in the morning and an appearance in the evening, and was sleeping in.

Nora Lowe paid no attention to the grogginess in Marion's voice: "Marion, I'm throwing a big party tonight. You have to come."

"I don't have the energy to go out tonight. I was out late last night."

"Ann Mark's brother is here from Ottawa. He's a good friend and I want you to meet him."

Nora prided herself on being the first person whom Chinese of her generation would call when visiting from out of town. Nora knows *everybody,* people said, acknowledging as well that she liked nothing more than to bring people together. And so when Ann, a married friend, mentioned that her brother, Hin Lew, was in from Ottawa to visit their aged mother, Nora's party planning kicked into gear. Is your brother married yet? Nora asked. No, he was still a bachelor.

"I can't go, Nora. I'm too busy."

That was not how Nora regarded life; not even Marion Lim could be too busy for a party. Life was meant to be full. Nora's widowed mother had raised her to keep occupied; she and her eight siblings, besides public school, had private tutoring in Chinese and lessons in piano, music theory, violin, swimming and figure skating (with a chauffeur to ferry them to and from). While studying at UBC, Nora had found time for flying lessons. "The in-between times are for partying" was her motto. She and her husband, Harvey Lowe, the "Yo-yo King," had a house designed for entertaining, with a ballroom that could accommodate one hundred. It had a sprung wood floor and a fully stocked bar.

"I'm not hanging up until you say yes."

Marion knew if she said no and rang off, the telephone was only going to ring again.

"WE'RE GOING TO HAVE TO find you a Japanese girl!"

Hin Lew's friends said it only half-teasingly. They were concerned. Their career physicist friend had shown little interest in shedding his bachelorhood, something they each had taken care of long ago. At this rate, they told each other, no girl we know is going to be left.

Sixteen years earlier, in 1942, when Hin first arrived in Ottawa, the Chinese friends he made were mostly younger than him. They were of a generation still registering firsts: that year Robert (Kuey) Wong became the first offspring of Ottawa's Chinese families to graduate from university, earning a commerce degree from Queen's University. When Hin completed his undergraduate studies at UBC in 1940, a total of eighteen Chinese students were enrolled at the university.

At first, Hin had regarded Ottawa as only a hiatus between his master's degree and his doctorate. Yet, in leaving Vancouver, the city of his birth, other than return visits every few years to his sisters and mother, he sensed he was leaving the west coast behind for good. The reason was the exhilaration he'd felt on coming east at encountering less discrimination in Toronto, and when he made the move to Ottawa, less again. In Toronto, he'd been emboldened enough to take out a white girl;

nobody speared him with a censorious look. In Ottawa he found attitudes among Chinese and whites alike to be even more relaxed. He'd wondered at the time if those war years would be the best in his life, when he boarded with the kindly Mrs. Cowan and her family in Old Ottawa South off Bank Street; she'd bake his favourite pie, apple custard, and he'd help her clean up in the kitchen while they chatted.

Hin did his part for Canada's war effort, working for the National Research Council on the use of ultrasound to detect submarines, experimenting in the Ottawa River right behind the NRC's building. At the end of the war, he left to pursue his doctorate at the Massachusetts Institute of Technology. Four years later, he returned to the Research Council to resume working alongside one of the world's leading molecular physicists. Dr. Gerhard Herzberg had first come to Canada when he'd been forced from his academic post in Nazi Germany because his wife, Luisa Dettinger, was Jewish.

The biggest difference Hin found from his earlier time in Ottawa was the livelier social scene among unmarried Chinese. Young people in Ottawa, Montreal and Toronto organized weekend excursions and exchanges and trips away. Ottawa's appeal had much to do with the fun-loving Taiwanese ambassador who hosted parties and balls at the embassy residence. A golfer, he often invited the Chinese youth to be his guests at the Royal Ottawa Golf Club, where, he pointed out—not without some smugness—Chinese were welcomed as club members but Jews were not.

The children of Chinese families in Ottawa had always taken it as a given that they'd have to look elsewhere else for their wife or husband. We've grown up together, they said. We're like sisters and brothers. Not only was the community very small, but certain surnames predominated. As the Chinese saying went, "You don't cook beef with beef." Other unspoken biases narrowed their choices. In the way that those who learned to play bridge henceforth eschewed the game of mahjong, on one side of a divide were café owners, on the other laundrymen. Or, on one side, Canadian-born Chinese, and on the other, newer immigrants who'd come after exclusion, via Hong Kong.

But while courtships among Ottawa's Chinese families were the exception, on Hin's return he was mesmerized by one girl, Bernice, whose parents, Stanley and Marion Wong, owned the Canton Inn restaurant. Descended from Irish grandparents on her mother's side, the fair-skinned Bernice thought she didn't look Chinese at all. What mattered to her many Chinese suitors was that she was uncommonly pretty, and she had charm to go with her beauty.

On group cycling trips to the Gatineau Hills, Hin would try to manoeuvre his bike to ride alongside her, all the while noticing the sidelong glances of every other male. Bernice was only sixteen, still in high school, and Ottawa's youth adhered to doing everything in a group, from cycling and hiking to skiing and skating. Still, Hin made his move. He secured two tickets to a performance of the famed Sadler's Wells Ballet on the Ottawa stop of their debut North American tour, featuring Margot Fonteyn in *Sleeping Beauty,* and invited Bernice. She readily accepted. The two paired off frequently after that within the group, and Hin also tutored her in subjects at school. However, a year later, when Bernice left for McGill University, Hin lost out to a rival from Ottawa who was enrolled at McGill. Norman Sim, one of the five Sim boys, and brother of restaurateur Jack, was in his second year studying enginerring there.

In Montreal, Bernice was as much at home as she was in Ottawa. Her father had been a chef and her mother the maid for a Montreal widow of a captain with the Cunard Line. A generous woman, the widow had given Bernice and her parents their own spacious quarters in her Westmount mansion. When Bernice was young, she and her father would walk through McGill's Roddick Gates, sometimes stopping to watch the players on the tennis courts. One day, her father pointed to the stately Moyse Hall and the arts building, and said to her, "Maybe someday you can go there."

After Norman and Bernice were married in 1955, their friends, married and single, Hin among them, continued to drop by her parents' home in Old Ottawa South in the evenings. They liked the refinement of Stanley Wong's hospitality, including his offers of liqueurs. Hin was content, untroubled that he was approaching his mid-thirties, unmarried. He was absorbed in his work at the Research Council, where not a day went by that Dr. Herzberg—a future Nobel Laureate—didn't think they were on the brink of a scientific breakthrough. Hin devoted himself to constructing an atomic and molecular beam laboratory, for which the Research Council had provided an empty room measuring thirty feet by thirty feet.

"I'M NOT GOING TO line up all night. I'm a bachelor!"

Hin could not be convinced. Jou-Juoh Lee—"JJ" to his friends—had joined with four friends and was trying to persuade him of a deal that he was certain wouldn't come around again. Among those friends, Leslie Wong was in real estate and ought to know.

At nine the next morning at the downtown office of the Crown corporation Central Mortgage and Housing, three hundred lots in Riverview subdivision at Ottawa's eastern edge would go on sale on a first-come, first-served basis, for two hundred and fifty dollars. The catch was that buyers had to sign a mortgage with the agency for a thousand dollars, to be forgiven if the purchaser built within two years. The agency also designated the type of house—bungalow, one and a half storey, or two storey—depending on the lot. The bargain, said JJ, was in the lot. They were fully serviced; the going price for such lots was two thousand dollars. The agency, set up to stimulate house building in anticipation of the baby boom, had heavily promoted the Ottawa sale in newspapers and on radio. Sure that the lots would be snapped up, JJ and his friends decided to spend the night in line.

Hin declared that he would not be participating. "I'm quite happy being a tenant. I don't see that as a single man I have need of a house. And I don't want the hassle of hiring and dealing with a contractor."

But he laid out why JJ should go ahead: his future was securely in Ottawa, since he had a good job at the Department of National Defence; and he was in a serious relationship that looked headed for marriage. JJ was dating Helen Way-nee. Now divorced, Helen had returned to Ottawa from abroad, to help her aged mother care for June, Helen's disabled sister.

Like Hin, JJ was not from Ottawa. The two had met at MIT, where JJ, the son of a county governor in China, attended on a full scholarship. The others—Leslie Wong, the realtor, Donald Sim, a lawyer and another of Jack's brothers, and brothers Eddie and Bill Joe, one an engineer and the other a restaurateur, were born to Ottawa's pioneer families. None had stayed in the family business; where once they'd lived in the back of a laundry or above a café in downtown Ottawa or Hull, now they aspired to a suburban home. One could imagine a family life where they'd meet their children's teachers, help with their homework, read *The Night Before Christmas* aloud together on Christmas Eve—things that their parents, at the mercy of their businesses and struggling with English, didn't have time for or couldn't do.

That evening, Hin retired to his own bed.

Early the next morning, he was woken by the telephone. It was JJ. "You can still get in on the sale if you hurry down here." Apparently, some in line had changed their minds, including two of their friends. Hin roused himself and headed downtown.

NORA STRESSED TO Hin that, excluding herself and Ann as the hosts, all thirty guests at the party—fifteen men, fifteen women—were "eligible."

As always, in drawing up her invitation lists, Nora gave careful thought as to which individuals might pair off. She could take credit for at least three introductions that had led to marriages. She decided that Marion Lim and Hin Lew, both fiercely determined people, were a match. Marion's determination was legendary; everybody remembered how hard she had worked at learning English. As for Hin, he'd realized his dream of going to university on years of his and his mother's scrimping and saving. His father had turned the success of his various businesses into ruin, dying penniless and leaving Hin's mother to raise four young children. In the summers, the youngster Hin worked alongside her, snipping the ends off string beans and weeding between the rows at a market garden. In his teen years, he toiled in canneries up the B.C. coast. His sister, Ann, had a job at a Chinese produce store and at day's end, brought home yellowed vegetables not fit for sale. To save bus fare during his four years at UBC, Hin rode his used one-speed bicycle to and from their house in Chinatown and the campus, six miles each way.

Nora realized there was an age difference between Marion and Hin of twelve years. That was for them to decide if it mattered. Certainly it didn't show. Nora thought they'd make a handsome couple, both slender, tall and graceful.

Hin told himself that one had to admire Nora for achieving a balance of single women and men, and in such numbers. He thought about possible outcomes. No one has to come with any intentions, he decided. This is just a social gathering; one can hope for suitable collisions.

AFTER HIN'S VISIT TO Vancouver, he and Marion corresponded. Smitten with her, Hin felt self-conscious about his ability to use English expressively. He could write scientific papers of an international calibre, but he was afraid his English lacked elegance. He need not have feared.

Of Hin's spoken English, Marion would say it was "perfect." She thought the written English in his letters confirmed the precision with which he spoke. Completely surprising was his penmanship and fluency in Chinese, a few lines of which he included in every letter. She felt humbled that she, with seven years of schooling in China, should be impressed by how someone born and raised in Canada presented himself in what was her mother tongue.

IN NOVEMBER OF 1959, after their wedding in Vancouver the year after they'd first met, Marion readied to leave with Hin for their new home in Ottawa—one that Hin had designed himself in the Riverview subdivision. In packing for the east, she made sure to shop for an extra-warm coat for Ottawa winters. She had yet to experience sub-zero temperatures and snow. Once there, she was dismayed to find that even in her new wool coat, her teeth rattled and she shook against the cold.

Several months later, in defiance of the last lingering patches of snow, a warming sun coaxed out the first crocuses, the purple and yellow and white flowers cheerily announcing spring. When Marion observed people shedding their winter wear in favour of lighter-weight coats, she realized that the coat she'd been wearing all winter was ill-chosen, more suited perhaps to the spring weather. A smile crossed her face. She was thinking of that awkward evening when she'd worn the coral-coloured tiered gown; such missteps were all part of finding one's way.

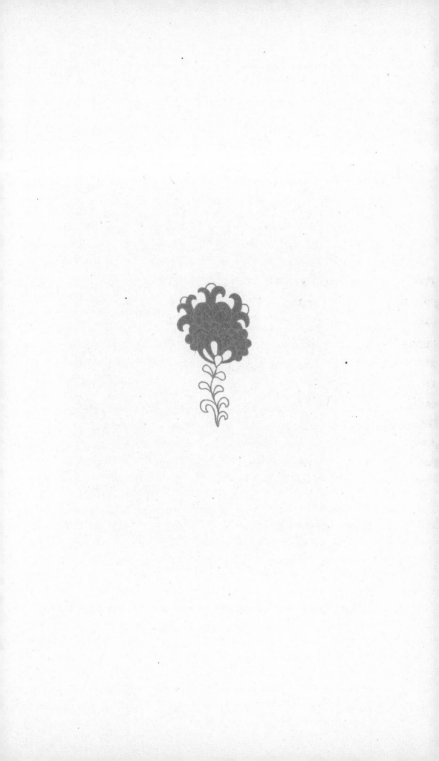

See-fat Hum in China, one year after his release from prison.
Courtesy Lui-sang Wong

TWELVE

ARRIVAL $\left(2\right)$

AFTER A DECADE LIVING downtown on Waverley Street, Lui-sang and Tsan Wong enjoyed the quiet of their home in the Glebe, a sedate, leafy Ottawa neighbourhood of large, older brick homes set back from the street, an area pleasantly dotted with parks adjoining the Rideau Canal.

In 1979, their lives were about to change again, in a way they'd hoped for but hardly imagined possible. Thirteen years earlier, Lui-sang had sponsored her mother, Hoi-sui, to come to Canada. As early as a year from now, in 1980—depending on the progress of the paperwork in China—they would add another member to their household: Lui-sang's father, See-fat. After thirty years in prison, he had finally been released.

On the eve of her departure for China, where she would return to the village to visit her husband, Hoi-sui sat her daughter and son-in-law down for a serious chat. She wanted them to understand her intentions once she got to China.

Officials at the Chinese embassy in Ottawa had assured the family that Hoi-sui should have no problems. Go and visit the village, they told her. Get your husband to fill out the form to apply to emigrate from China to Canada. Then, come back to Canada and wait. "These things take time," they said.

Hoi-sui confessed her fears. Why had it taken two tries, two applications, before the embassy had granted her a visa so that she could visit her husband? Maybe China's Communist government had released See-fat but had not declared him "rehabilitated," so that he still carried the label of capitalist and landlord. Maybe prison authorities would change their minds, and would yet send him back to the forced labour camp at the mine in the Mongolian mountains.

Tsan and Lui-sang admitted to being nervous themselves that authorities would deny See-fat permission to leave China. If the government didn't object on political grounds, what if local officials were swayed by greed: as long as he remained there, his family in Canada would keep sending money. The couple didn't know what to make of a recent letter that See-fat had smuggled out to them. Apparently, every time the postman showed up at his door, neighbours came asking for money. Some well-meaning villagers had suggested that maybe it was better that his family not send him any money: "They said that our family could be hurt, like before." Even in tiny script, on such a small piece of paper—presumably easier to conceal—See-fat hadn't been able to write much.

Hoi-sui couldn't help but fear for her own safety. Could authorities still hold it against her that she'd escaped from the country? Even now, more than twenty years since she'd fled with her three young children, "What if they say, how did you get to Canada? We didn't let you out." In 1978, the world had hailed China's momentous change of policy, its new "Open Door" to the west. Still, Hoi-sui was afraid; had the authorities released her husband only to lure her back?

None of the three had any answers.

Hoi-sui told them she had her plane ticket, so there would be no second thoughts about going. But she wanted her daughter to know she had made up her mind: "If they don't let me return to Canada or if they don't let your father out—either way—I will stay with him." He was sixty-one; she was fifty-eight. As husband and wife, they had already missed most of a lifetime to be together.

Lui-sang and Tsan told nothing of this to their three sons. They didn't want them to worry that they might never see their grandmother again; she'd lived with the family since before two of them were even born. Canada, and more particularly Ottawa, was the only home they'd known. Yet if everything went as planned and events came full circle, they would begin to understand what it means to have an immigrant past. They'd see that for the migrant, to leave one shore and to arrive at another is neither the beginning nor the end. If they should be so lucky, they'd become part of the calculus of their grandfather's negotiation between the familiar and the strange, the old and the new. And perhaps one day, when the time came to write themselves into the narrative of the lives of the family, they would see that even a lifetime isn't the end of the tale.

As far as the Wongs' three boys, Harvey, Howard and Vincent, were concerned, Grandma was going to visit her husband and he was going to come to Canada to live with them. The youngest, Vincent, aged nine, wondered which room his grandfather would end up taking, if he or one of his brothers would have to give up their space.

Adrienne (centre) and Neville Poy (right) with friends
in the backyard of the Poys' first home in Ottawa.
Courtesy Adrienne Clarkson

EPILOGUE

THE WRITER Ursula Le Guin ends her 1979 essay on narrative, "It Was a Dark and Stormy Night: Or, Why Are We Huddling About the Campfire?" with a story that, as she explains in her concluding comments, has been retold by a boy:

> But by remembering it he had made the story his; and insofar as I have remembered it, it is mine; and now if you like it, it's yours. In the tale, in the telling, we are all one blood. . . . [W]e will all come to the end together, even to the beginning: living as we do, in the middle.

The tales in these pages of the immigrant's life are a tribute to life lived in the middle—finding one's bearings while longing for home, remaking one's future while wrestling with memory.

These being the final pages, I leave the reader with a brief return visit to some of the people in these stories.

See-fat Hum arrived three years after his wife's visit to China to a greeting party of thirty family and friends at the Ottawa Airport. His grandson Harvey would write a high-school composition about the meeting entitled "A Night to Remember."

Eva Devlin, whom Doris Johnston worked with at the Perth Shoe Factory, realized her ambition of earning a pilot's licence and owning a small airplane. On the afternoon of September 15, 1949, Eva was to take Doris for her first-ever plane ride and show her Perth from the air. At the last minute, a large party of Americans arrived to dine at Harry's Cafe and, reluctantly, Doris cancelled her date with Eva. Eva took to the skies, but on making her approach to land, her plane went into a spin, nose-dived into the ground and disintegrated on impact.

Mabel Johnston, who took over Harry's Café in 1940, was a millionaire by the time of her death in 1965.

The girl who ran away from Barry's Bay, only to be turned back by old Mr. Lang in Carp, hitchhiked all the way to Vancouver a few months later.

Golden Lang stood by during his Christmas holidays in 1971 to develop the first photographs taken of the baby born to Prime Minister Pierre Trudeau and his wife, Margaret, a son whom they named Justin.

Jasper Hum's widow, Margaret, was given back her husband's house when the Chinese government began returning confiscated property after 1979. She offered it to her niece, Shui-dan. Shui-dan didn't want it, saying that it held too many bad memories for her.

Marion (née Lim) Lew saw her mother again in China after thirty-two years, in 1982. She decided to ask her mother, before the answer was lost to the grave, if she was of mixed blood. Her mother said only that, while pregnant with Marion, she'd seen a beautiful white child and had kept the image uppermost in her mind.

Agnes Lor was named Brockville's "Citizen of the Year" in 1984. Her son, Joe, likes to think of her as the first feminist he knew.

Adrienne Clarkson, the youngest child of the Poy family, to whom the Canadian government granted refugee status, achieved the exceptional and became Canada's twenty-sixth governor general, a posting she held from 1999 to 2005.

Gertrude Hum, widowed in 2005 from her husband, Joe, who'd once formed a study group of Chinese students at Lisgar Collegiate, had "B. Comm." engraved on her husband's tombstone, knowing how proud he was of his degree.

Lai-sim Leung fulfilled her dream and in 1968 bought the Capital Café, later renaming it the Ging Sing, in Ottawa. In part, she did it to provide work for some of her five newly arrived relatives from Hong Kong. In 2005, she lost the business when fire consumed the building. At first devastated, Lai-sim later had an epiphany: "I am free now."

Of course, depending on how one holds the tapestry of life up to the light, different threads can catch one's attention. I wove them into stories I made mine, but now they are yours.

ACKNOWLEDGEMENTS

I OWE THE ORIGINS OF this book to the community spirit of the Ottawa Chinese Community Service Centre (OCCSC), a non-profit organization, which since 1975 has provided settlement services to newcomers, immigrants and refugees. Among its founders were children of Ottawa Chinese pioneers, including William (Bill) Joe. His childhood home, Joe's Laundry & Cleaners, featured on this book's cover, was a place where new arrivals could count on a meal and a place to rest their head. In 2011, the OCCSC received a modest grant from the government of Canada under a program of redress for the head tax, to create an educational website on the history of Ottawa-area Chinese pioneers. The OCCSC commissioned me to develop that website, LivesOfTheFamily.com. As I delved into my research, I was struck by the tenacity of individuals, often against the odds dealt by history and politics. From there, my idea for a book of linked stories on a theme of the lives of immigrant families in small-town Canada took root on the enthusiasm of my agent, Jackie Kaiser, and Anne Collins and Craig Pyette of Random House Canada. My life is enriched by three such thoughtful individuals, each passionate about their work. I feel fortunate to be an author with Random House Canada.

When I began this book, early Chinese cafés and businesses in the Ottawa area had mostly passed into history. The second generation of families who'd settled here was giving way to a third. I am grateful for the generosity of each and every family member who shared memories with me. I was privileged: many, if not most, were giving voice to their memories for the first time. My appreciation goes to families and individuals in these pages and on the website, and many more whom I interviewed and on whose experience I drew. You faced my endless questions, you dusted off family albums and pulled out shoe boxes of photographs and documents, you laughed, you wept. Some were teachers to me: the late Harry Sim, Robert Hum, the late Doris Soong, Joe Lor and Hin Lew. Linda Hum and Arlene Lang accompanied me to their hometowns. Lui-sang Wong, Lai-sim Leung and Marion Hum fed me. I owe thanks to friends that families made before they arrived in Ottawa, and who shared their recollections with me. I include among them Eric Devlin, Jeanne Yuen, Earl Dick, Ann Parsons, Nora Loe and Freda Lim.

Thank you to those who lent photographs for my research, with special mention to Hin Lew. Photographs are reprinted here by permission. Along with video clips, many more can be viewed on the website. At the OCCSC's launch of that website, Robert Hum, Bill Joe, Joe Lor, Neville Poy and Gladys Wong gave mesmerizing accounts of life lived behind or above the family business and of their childhoods during and after the Second World War.

On sources, I benefited from an unpublished essay by Professor Jean-Guy Daigle of the University of Ottawa, written in 2000, entitled "From Survival to Success: The Chinese in

Twentieth-Century Ottawa." I wish to acknowledge private memoirs or writing by Joe Hum, Marion Lew and Harvey Wong. I drew upon the website "Chinese-Canadian Women 1923–1967: Inspiration, Innovation, Ingenuity" (mhso.ca/ChineseCanadianWomen) produced by the Multicultural History Society of Ontario. I relied on Valerie Mah's speech "The Chinese Shop in the Canadian Context" to the "Counter Cultures" conference at Ryerson University in 2011. The excerpt from Ruth Lor's letter to her mother in "Outcomes" is reprinted with her permission. The song "Marianne" quoted in "Life" topped the charts in 1957 in the recording by Terry Gilkyson and the Easy Riders. The quotation in the epilogue from Ursula Le Guin is from "It Was a Dark and Stormy Night: Or, Why Are We Huddling About the Campfire?" a paper she presented at a symposium on narrative at the University of Chicago in 1979.

I wish to pay tribute to the leadership, support and camaraderie of a group that came together under the aegis of the OCCSC: Bill Joe, Jonas Ma, Sharon Kan, Yew Lee, Robert Yip and Albert Tang, who were committed to seeing through a project to safeguard a place in the historical record for Ottawa-area Chinese families as part of the story of Canada. The well from which I drew stories for this book is bottomless; many more stories are there for the telling.

I dedicate this book to Diana Lary, a scholar of Chinese history. I benefit from her wisdom and learn much from all her books, including her recent work, *The Chinese People at War: Human Suffering and Social Transformation, 1937–1945* (Cambridge University Press, 2010). Diana is a dear friend and a mentor.

I cannot thank my mother enough: she was always ready on e-mail and at the end of the telephone, prepared to canvass her friends, to answer my questions about Chinese language, traditions and food. And, thank you with love to my husband, Roger, and my children, Jade and Kai. "How's the writing going, Mom" was encouragement enough.

DENISE CHONG is the author of *The Concubine's Children*, a family memoir; *The Girl in the Picture*, a story of the napalm girl from the Vietnam War; and *Egg on Mao*, a portrayal of human rights in China. She lives with her family in Ottawa. In 2013, she was made an Officer of the Order of Canada.